# CLASSIC SERMONS
## ON THE
# SECOND COMING
## AND OTHER PROPHETIC THEMES

Compiled by
Warren W. Wiersbe

*Classic Sermons on the Second Coming and other Prophetic Themes*
Hendrickson Publishers, Inc. edition
ISBN 1-56563-072-6

This edition is published by special arrangement with and permission of Kregel Publications. 

*Printed in the United States of America*

# CONTENTS

## SCRIPTURE TEXT INDEX

# PREFACE

THE *KREGEL CLASSIC SERMONS SERIES* is an attempt to assemble and publish meaningful sermons from master preachers about significant themes.

These are *sermons*, not essays or chapters taken from books about themes. Not all of these sermons could be called "great," but all of them are *meaningful*. They apply the truths of the Bible to the needs of the human heart, which is something that all effective preaching must do.

While some are better known than others, all of the preachers, whose sermons I have selected, had important ministries and were highly respected in their day. The fact that a sermon is included in this volume does not mean that either the compiler or the publisher agrees with or endorses everything that the man did, preached, or wrote. The sermon is here, because it has a valued contribution to make.

These are sermons about *significant* themes. The pulpit is no place to play with trivia. The preacher has thirty minutes in which to help mend broken hearts, change defeated lives, and save lost souls; and he can never accomplish this demanding ministry by distributing homiletical tidbits. In these difficult days; we do not need "clever" pulpiteers who discuss the times; we need dedicated ambassadors who will preach the eternities.

The reading of these sermons can enrich your own spiritual life. The studying of them can enrich your own skills as an interpreter and expounder of God's truth. However God uses these sermons in your own life and ministry, my prayer is that His Church around the world will be encouraged and strengthened by them.

WARREN W. WIERSBE

## Second Coming of Christ

**William Ashley ("Billy") Sunday** (1862-1935) was the most popular, and probably the most fruitful, evangelist in America during the first three decades of the twentieth century. A professional baseball player from 1883 to 1891, Sunday was converted to Christ in 1886, and five years later went to work with the YMCA in Chicago. From 1893 to 1895, he served with evangelist J. Wilbur Chapman, and in 1896 launched out on his own as a full-time evangelist. Sunday was ordained into the Presbyterian ministry in 1903 and two years later started his city-wide evangelistic campaigns. His preaching style was considered sensational, if not theatrical; but he attracted huge crowds and was used of God to win an estimated three hundred thousand sinners to faith in Christ.

"The Second Coming of Christ" was reported in the *Omaha (NE) Daily News* on October 1, 1915, and reprinted in volume 7 of *20 Centuries of Great Preaching*, edited by Clyde E. Fant, Jr. and William M. Pinson, Jr., and published by Word Books, Waco, Texas.

William Ashley ("Billy") Sunday

# 1

# SECOND COMING OF CHRIST

> Then we which are alive and remain shall be caught up together with them in the clouds, to meet the Lord in the air; and so shall we ever be with the Lord. Wherefore comfort one another with these words (1 Thessalonians 4:17-18).

THE MEETING HERE mentioned is to be the greatest meeting the Bible tells us anything about.

There have been some wonderful meetings, but never has there been one to compare with this. It was a wonderful meeting the children of Isràel had on the shore of the Red Sea, after Pharaoh's pursuing host had been destroyed in the angry waters, and Miriam, the prophetess, with her timbrel, led the people in singing, "Sing ye to the Lord, for he hath triumphed gloriously: the horse and his rider hath he thrown into the sea" (Ex. 15:21).

And it was another great meeting they had at the foot of Mount Sinai, when the law of God was given to them and thunders and lightnings and fire and smoke.

That was a great meeting, too, on Mount Carmel, when Elijah, the sturdy Tishbite, defied the prophets of Baal; and that was a great meeting where David danced before the ark of God, as it was borne into Jerusalem.

It was a great meeting when Solomon dedicated the temple, and the glory of the Lord came upon the people, and those were great meetings that were held on the banks of the Jordan when Jerusalem and all Judea went out to hear the man who dressed in camel's hair and wore a linen girdle, and lived on locusts and wild honey.

It was a wonderful meeting when Jesus preached the Sermon on the Mount, and another when He fed the multitude with five loaves and two fishes. And that was a great meeting on the day of Pentecost, when the Spirit came like a rushing mighty wind, and under Peter's preaching about three thousand were converted.

All these were great meetings, and any number of others have been held, both in former times and in our own day.

Those were great meetings in the early days of Methodism, when Wesley and Whitefield preached to great multitudes in the fields. Those were great meetings when multitudes were flocking to hear Finney and Moody; and great meetings have since been held by other great evangelists all around the world.

But no meeting has ever been held anywhere or in any time that could begin to compare in importance with the greatest of all meetings that is to be held in the air, when our Lord comes to make up His jewels.

That meeting is the one for which all others have been preparing the way. It will be the crowning meeting of all history. The purpose of all that has been done in this world up to the present times has been to prepare for that great meeting in the air.

From Adam, mankind has been marching step by step up a grand stairway leading direct to that meeting in the air. The call of Abraham was one step toward it, and Jacob and his twelve sons were another. Joseph ruling Egypt was another; the deliverance under Moses another; the conquest of Canaan under Joshua another, and so on with every event in sacred history.

It was for this Jesus suffered on the cross to make atonement for sin. It was for this He arose from the dead and ascended into heaven, where He took His place at the right hand of the Father. It was for this the Holy Spirit came at Pentecost, and it was for this that churches have been organized and missionaries sent to the ends of the earth.

These things have all been done to prepare the way, and lead up to the meeting which is so graphically described in the text.

It was for this meeting God made His plans before He laid the foundations of the earth, and it was of this meeting He was thinking before the morning stars sang together.

We are not told when Jesus will come, but we are told that His coming is sure, and we are charged to watch for it.

Anybody who says that he knows when Jesus is coming is a liar. When they say that they know when He is coming they lie. Only the Father knows when the Savior is coming again.

Yet the church today shows as little concern about His coming again as His disciples did about His going away. All this is fully in accord with Peter: "There shall come in the last days scoffers walking after their own lusts, saying, Where is the promise of his coming, for since the fathers fell asleep all things continue as they were from the beginning until now?" (2 Peter 3:3-4).

Jesus not only foretold His going away, but charged His followers to expect His return, and be ready for it: "Watch, therefore, for ye know not what hour your Lord doth come. Therefore, be ye also ready, for in such an hour as ye think not the son of man cometh" (Matt..24:42-44).

Every time we lift the communion cup to our lips we "do show forth the Lord's death till he come." There is no prophecy needing to be fulfilled before Christ comes. Jesus said: "This gospel of the kingdom shall be preached in all the world for a witness unto all nations; then shall the end come" (Matt. 24:14).

Before I started to preach in Omaha, God knew the names of every man, woman and child who would be saved as a result of my preaching. If God didn't know that, He wouldn't be God.

And God knew all about the fools who wouldn't be saved, and He knew that all of Omaha wouldn't be saved.

I tell you that God is pretty wise to who are going to hell and who are going to heaven. The sooner you get that through your head and don't try to sidestep Jesus, the sooner the devil will let go the stranglehold he has upon most of you.

There is not a nation on the earth that has not had the gospel preached within its bounds.

The second coming of Christ is the emphatic doctrine of the New Testament. It is mentioned and referred to more than 350 times, and yet the majority of church members never heard a sermon on the subject; that is the reason they think so little of looking into the matter themselves.

The church makes much of baptism, but in all of Paul's epistles baptism is only mentioned or referred to thirteen times, while the return of the Lord is mentioned fifty times. This certainly shows which he considered the most important.

McCheyne, the great Scotch preacher, once said to some of his friends: "Do you think Christ will come back tonight?"

One after another they said: "I think not."

Then he solemnly repeated: "Watch, therefore, for ye know not what hour your Lord doth come. Therefore, be ye also ready, for in such an hour as ye think not the son of man cometh" (Matt. 24:42-44).

With such admonitions as this, what right have we to be unconcerned about it and say, as many preachers do, "It is nothing to me; I take no interest in the subject, whatever"?

Who would care to travel on a train where the engineer would never read his orders? Who would ride on a ship where the captain never looked at the compass? You may call it rubbish, but the disciples called it the "blessed hope."

"Why call ye me Lord, Lord, and do not the things I say?" If Jesus had said: "I will not return for 2,000 years," nobody would have begun to look for Him before the time was near, but He expects His followers to be always looking for His return. Just as Simeon and Anna watched and waited for His coming, so we should be watching and waiting for His return.

It is not enough to say, "Oh, I'm a Christian; I'm all right."

We are not all right unless we obey the command to watch, for it is certainly as much of a command to look for the coming of the Lord as it is to keep the Sabbath holy. Nothing else will do so much to keep us right where we should be in our religious experience.

Knowing that the bank examiner may drop in at any moment keeps many a cashier from becoming dishonest.

We should purify the church that it may be the proper

bride to meet the Lord in the air. How pure is the church today? How pure are the church members? How pure are the preachers?

I suppose there would be a mighty scramble to get right with God if you all found out that Jesus was going to return tonight. It wouldn't make any difference to Jesus if you had to do the right thing just because He turned up unexpectedly. You would have to prove to Him that you were on the level with Him, and although you might all be baptized, sprinkled and immersed, there would be nothing doing in the salvation line if you didn't play square with the Lord.

This old world is going to wake up some morning and find that all good men and women have beaten it, and she'll rub her eyes when she finds out that the Lord has been here on the job and taken His own with Him.

Every time I preach and every time you do personal work, I feel that we are helping to bring about the second coming of the Lord, and it sets my bones on fire when I think that the last man or woman need only be saved before this campaign is over in order that the Lord may come.

That is my incentive to do the work I am doing. It is my hope that, before I finish here, the church will be purified as a bride, ready to meet Jesus, the bridegroom in the air.

A little more than twenty years ago Mr. Moody called a convention of Christian workers to meet in Chicago, and that convention was in session there in Moody's church for two months, and out of it came the great Bible institute.

The daily program was to spend the forenoon at the church in prayer and Bible study, and the afternoon and evening in doing practical Christian work.

A man who was my assistant some years ago attended that convention. He told me that one day Mr. Moody asked him to go down among the anarchists, in the hard parts of Chicago, and hold a meeting there.

"Do the best you can," said Moody, "and some night I'll come down and help you."

My friend said that promise was a continual incentive to him to keep up his courage and do his very best. He didn't know when Mr. Moody would come, and so he looked for him every night, and the harder time he had, the harder he hoped and looked.

This shows how the constant expectation of the coming of Jesus will inspire and encourage us.

A great many say: "I believe the millennium will come first, then Christ will come at the end of it." What people think has nothing to do with it, but what God says has everything to do with it.

Many have missed railroad trains because they believed they would come at a time that did not correspond with the official time card.

You will see God's time card if you carefully read the Bible. Not a word can be found in the Bible that gives the slightest hope for the millennium before the return of Christ; but you can find plenty of verses that tell you to look for the coming of the Lord first.

As we look back over the 2,000 years since Christ, how far we seem to be away from the time when the will of God shall be done on earth as it is in heaven. Every edition of the press seems to make it clear that the devil is still having his way.

Look at the reign of wickedness in our great cities in both high life and low. No college has ever yet made a saint or ever will. Education may improve conditions, but it can never change or cleanse the heart.

Look at the lukewarmness and indifference in the churches everywhere and see what many of them are compelled to resort to in order to keep from going under. See to what schemes and dodges and foolishness some preachers have to resort to get anybody to go and hear them.

There can be no millennium until Jesus comes; it is His presence that makes the millennium. You might as well talk of daylight not coming until the sun goes down. The millennium cannot begin until Satan has been bound in the pit. Nothing is more certain than that the glory of God shall cover the earth, but it will be after Jesus comes.

Many have an idea the world will grow better and better until the coming of the millennium, and everybody will be converted, and you hear that stuff preached, but the Bible does not teach any such trash.

On the day before the flood there were no doubt many people who were sincere in thinking that the world was growing better, and yet it was so hopelessly wicked that God had to destroy it. Some of the men who married into the family of Lot may have made the same claim for Sodom, only a day or two before its destruction; no doubt Lot's wife was of the same opinion.

On the day before the crucifixion there were men in Jerusalem who undoubtedly agreed with each other that the world was growing better. The world will grow worse and worse. They did eat, they drank, they married wives, they were given in marriage until the day that Noah entered the ark and the flood came and destroyed them all.

Likewise also as it was in the days of Lot, they did eat, they drank, they bought, they sold, they planted, they built. But the same day that Lot went out of Sodom it rained fire and brimstone from heaven and destroyed them all.

"Even thus shall it be in the day when the son of man is revealed" (Luke 17:27-30). Lawlessness, vice and crime will increase; communism, nihilism, anarchy, adultery, divorce, graft, all will continue to grow until they will finally ripen into the anti-Christ.

Many think and preach that the millennium will be brought about by the increase of knowledge, culture, great discoveries, such as the gasoline engine, automobile, electricity, radium, liquified air, wireless telegraphy, airships, etc.

These have nothing to do with bringing in the millennium. It is the personal reign of Christ that brings the millennium. Those who have been the greatest blessing to the world were filled with this hope and preached it.

The Word of God was vitiated and neutralized by the traditions of men when Jesus first came, and that is very largely the trouble in present times. Instead of going to the Bible to find out what God says, the preacher is too apt to go to his books, to see what the great men of his church have to say about it, and all their preaching and teaching take its color from the glasses the rabbis wear, just as was the case in the time of Jesus.

The fact that Jesus was not recognized by the high-up authorities, but was rejected and crucified as an impostor, shows what a dangerous and deadly thing it is to accept the traditions of men rather than what God says about things.

Too many who are now masters in Israel are as much in the dark as Nicodemus was. The truth is no harder to get at than a corn on the cob, if we will first strip off the husk and shell it. We need to depend more upon the Holy Spirit and less upon our libraries if we would preach so that those who hear us will also hear the voice of God in our message.

It is not what the Doctor This or Professor That has to say about it that settles the question, and settles it right, but who reads the Word. What does the Bible say about it? And what we need to do is to take the Bible as it reads, not as some big man says it means.

Big men have been mistaken about vital things just about as often as little ones. The safest pilot is not the one who wears the biggest hat, but the one who knows the channel the best. We should let the Bible speak to us just as God means it should, without distorting it by the prejudices and vagaries of those who are always trying to put their own camel into it and strain out somebody else's gnat.

It is high time for Christians to interpret unfulfilled prophecies by the light of prophecies already fulfilled.

The curses on the Jews were brought to pass literally; so also will be the blessings.

The scattering was literal; so also will be the gatherings.

The pulling down of Zion was literal; and so also must be the restoration.

The first coming of Christ was literal, visible and personal, and what right has anybody to conclude that His second coming will be altogether spiritual? If His first advent was with a real body, why not the same with His second coming?

When Jesus first came the smallest predictions were fulfilled to the very letter; and should this not teach us to expect that the same will be true when He comes again? There are very many more prophecies concerning His second coming than His first, and does not this mean that God wants to give us the most favorable opportunity possible to prepare for it? If the humility and shame of Christ at His first coming were literal and visible, should not His second coming in power and glory be also literal and visible?

What right have we to say that the words Judah, Zion, Israel and Jerusalem ever mean anything but literal Judah, Zion, Israel and Jerusalem? Someone has called attention to the fact that there are only two or three places in the whole New Testament where such names are used in what may be called a spiritual or figurative way.

Jerusalem occurs eighty times, and in every case is unquestionably literal, except when the opposite is clearly indicated by such qualifying terms as "heavenly," "new" or "holy." Jew occurs a hundred times, and only four are ambiguous. Israel and Israelite occur forty times, and all literal. Judah and Judea about twenty times, and literal in every case.

John Bunyan was once studying the passage foretelling that the feet of the Lord should stand on the Mount of Olives, and he thus reasoned:

"Some commentators say that the Mount of Olives means the heart of the believer; that is only a figurative expression, and means that the Lord will reign in the heart of the believer, and the Holy Spirit will dwell there. But I don't think it means that at all. I just think it means Mount of Olives, two miles from Jerusalem, on the east."

And that is why the Lord could use the poor tinker so marvelously, even when he was shut up in Bedford jail.

While face to face with them, Jesus taught His disciples to be in constant expectation of His early return, and they so understood Him and lived accordingly. They preached the doctrine and taught it in their epistles, every one of them. Certainly, if anybody ever understood the Lord correctly, it was the men whom He personally trained to do that very thing, that they might hand the truth He gave them down to us. If they failed to understand Him, what hope is there that anybody else may do so?

Jesus is going to come and reveal Himself to the members of His body at the very moment when the last soul is saved necessary to complete that body—for the body of Christ must consist of a certain number of souls, or it never could be completed.

If it were an infinite number, it would be an endless task, and Jesus would never return, for He can no more come with His heavenly body than He could come the first time without a human body. It is the completion of the body of Christ, therefore, that will bring Him, and this shows how we may help and hasten His coming.

"Looking for and hastening unto the coming of the day of the God wherein the heavens being on fire shall be dissolved and the elements shall melt with fervent heat" (2 Peter 3:12).

Every time we do personal work or try to get anybody saved, we may be doing something that will bring the coming of the Lord. Instead of being discouraged by looking about us and seeing what a small prospect there is of the whole world being converted, it will set our bones on fire to think that perhaps the last man needed to complete the Lord's body and bring Jesus back to earth may be converted this very day. That gives us something definite and tangible to work for, and hope for, don't you see?

Colonel Clark, the founder of the Pacific Garden mission in Chicago, put in six nights out of every seven at the mission as long as he lived. One day somebody said to him:

"Colonel, why don't you take some rest? You are killing yourself by sticking to that mission so close. Why don't you take a vacation and go away somewhere and rest?"

"I can't do it, brother," answered the colonel. "I could never do that, for every time I start for the mission, I think, maybe the last man may be saved in our little meeting tonight, and the Lord will come; and I wouldn't miss being at my post for anything in the world. When Jesus comes I want to be right where He expects me to be."

The Bible very clearly makes known the great truth that God's purpose for this dispensation is the completing of the body of Christ. He is not trying to save the world now; that is to be the work of the next dispensation. Here is the Scripture for it:

"God at the first did visit the Gentiles, to take out of them a people for His name. (The body of Christ.) And to this agree the words of the prophets; as it is written. After this I will return and will build again the tabernacle of David (the Jewish nation) which is fallen down (scattered and no longer being used); and I will build again the ruins thereof, and I will set them that the residue of men might seek after the Lord (through their missionary efforts)" (Acts 15:14-17).

That is the present dispensation, and that is what God is doing now. There is nothing said here about the conversion of the world, but it is made clear that a people is being chosen, and much Scripture might be quoted to show that the people so referred to will constitute the body of Christ.

Throughout this dispensation the Lord has been working among the Gentiles (those not belonging to the Jewish nation), and this shows the purpose for which He has been working. There is no thought expressed there of the millennium.

"And to this agree the words of the prophets (about God's purpose in gathering a chosen people from the Gentiles). As it is written (and that means what God says). After this (after the number of people to be chosen from the Gentiles has been fully completed) I will return (to direct dealing with Israel) and build again the tabernacle of David, which is fallen down" (Acts 15:15-16).

Fallen down. What does that mean? What does it mean for a house to be fallen down? Certainly that it cannot longer be used as a house while in that condition.

Read the prophecy of Amos, from which this is taken, and see why it is that God is through with Israel until He has taken from the Gentiles the people for His name. (To bear His name, to glorify His name.)

The mission of the church—the bride of Christ, or body of Christ—is to be ready to meet the bridegroom. When the body of Christ is completed He will reveal Himself to the members who are alive and in this world at that time, and at the same moment they will be caught up to meet those who have gone on before in the air, and from that moment they are forever with the Lord.

The body of Christ will be composed of believers from every race and nation on earth. That is why the gospel must first be preached as a witness to every nation. Not from every dispensation. It had its beginning on the day of Pentecost and will be complete at the time of the meeting in the air, which is called the rapture. For He is now preparing, perfecting and completing the church—the body of Christ, the bride who is to meet the Lord in the air, and be with Him forevermore.

These different members will be found, one here and another there, and gathered together from all parts of the world, and the moment the last one is saved Christ will be revealed—not to the world, but to His church—His bride—just as the electric light blazes out when the last condition is fulfilled. At that time Christ will not be revealed to the whole world, but only to the individual members of His body who may be alive and here at that time.

There remains no prophecy to be fulfilled. There is not a nation where the gospel has not been preached. So Christ must be waiting for the completion of the body of believers.

When the rapture comes it will come in the twinkle of an eye. Those who have died in the Lord will be resurrected, and they, with the believers who are alive, will be caught up to meet the Lord in the air.

When the rapture comes it will come in the twinkling of an eye, and will be altogether unexpected except by those who have been searching the prophecies and are looking for it, just as Simeon and Anna and the wise men were looking for Jesus at His first coming.

After it has occurred there will be an army of church

members and preachers who will not know that it has come, because they are not members of the Lord's body; for the Lord will not at that time be seen by any except those who have been caught up to meet Him in the air.

The remainder of the world will not know that He has been here, and they will not know what has become of the missing ones. They will seem to have disappeared in all kinds of unaccountable ways, unless their earthly bodies shall be left behind them, as the linen clothes of Jesus were left in the tomb. But things will soon settle back into their old condition, and the world go on its way, as did Sodom after Lot was taken out of it.

The notion that people have about the second coming of Christ is that when He comes the judgment day will also come, and that the world will come to an end. This idea is unscriptural and shows how little the Bible has been searched to find and make known the real truth by those who are leaders and teachers in the church.

Business will go on and governments will go on as now. After Jesus comes and takes the believers out of the world, then takes place the great tribulation, a description of which you will find later on. At the close of the tribulation the Lord will return, bringing with Him His saintly members of His body, to begin His millennium reign.

Then He will reveal Himself to the Jews. They will accept Him as their long-rejected Messiah. Then the millennium will begin; the devil will be cast into the bottomless pit for a thousand years; nations will be born in a day, through the missionary efforts of the Jews.

When the Jews accept Jesus Christ and bring to Him all their wonderful energy and intelligence, oh, this world will grow as it has never grown before! Nations will be born in a day.

The Jews have always been full of energy in business, as no other people, and when they become ambassadors for Christ there will be no lukewarmness or indifference. Either before or during the tribulation the Jews will have been restored to the holy land, rebuilding their temple and restoring the Jewish worship.

Also during the tribulation the anti-Christ will come,

most likely in the person of some great king. It is supposed that He will be a personal incarnation of the devil, just as Jesus was an incarnation of God.

He will go to Jerusalem, and there do great signs and wonders, by which He will so delude the chosen people that they will accept Him as their Messiah, and pay Him divine honors in the temple. It will be during this that Jesus will return and destroy Him by the brightness of His coming.

"And then shall the wicked be revealed, whom the Lord shall consume with the spirit of His mouth, and shall destroy with the brightness of His coming; even of Satan with all power and signs and lying wonders" (2 Thess. 2:8-9).

The devil has got some of you so close to hell that you can smell the fumes. He's no loafer. He's been working for 6,000 years, and he was never laid up with appendicitis nor tonsillitis, nor the grip.

In the Lord's coming there are to be two distinct phases—His coming for the members of His body, and the revelation to them at the time of the rapture, or taking up into the air, and His coming with the members of His body at the close of the tribulation, when He is revealed to the Jews and destroys the anti-Christ.

Overlooking these two places has put some people in confusion about the order of events, just as the failure to distinguish between the prophecies pertaining to the first and second coming confused the Jews, and caused them to reject Jesus, through what they supposed to be His failure to fulfill prophecy.

Yes, Christ will come in person, and will destroy the anti-Christ. The seat of his power will be Jerusalem. This is literal and not figurative.

The visible church will be left here, strong in members and organization. It will probably make a great show of missionary activity, but will have no more power against the principalities and powers of evil than did the disciples who missed the Mount of Transfiguration have over the demons that were tormenting the little boy.

In a worldly way it will appear to be in a very prosperous condition, rich in property and elegant buildings; but here is a picture of what it will be after the salt of the earth has been taken out of it:

"This know also that in the last days perilous times shall come. For men shall be lovers of their own selves, covetous, boasters, proud, blasphemers, disobedient to parents, unthankful, unholy, without natural affection; truce breakers, false accusers, inconsistent, fierce, despisers more than lovers of God, having a form of godliness but denying the power thereof" (2 Tim. 3:1-5).

Did you ever know a time in all history when the world was worse than it is now? People are passing up the church and the prayer meeting for the theater, the leg show and the movies. Oh, Lord, how we need someone to cry aloud, "Return to God."

Bear in mind that this has no reference to the Turks, the heathen in Africa or the people in the slums; but that it is a description of the rank and file of the church, after the Lord has come and taken His body out of the world. For notice that it is said that these people have a form of godliness which means that they are professors of religion. They are not avowed infidels or atheists, but professed believers.

Let us consider, in the first place, something of what it may mean to have a part in that meeting in the air:

1. Well, the most glorious thing about it is that if we are there we shall be members of the body of Jesus Christ. It will mean that we are members of the royal family of the universe; that we are kings and princes who are to sit on the throne and reign with Jesus, and that we shall be with Him forevermore, never to be separated from Him again.

And this will mean that we shall be the most exalted beings in all the universe, for who could be higher than the sons of God or the bride of our Lord?

We are living in the most important part of the world's history. Great heaven! I don't see how anyone can fail to be inspired.

It is an awful thing to miss being a part of the body of

Christ because you're too big a fool to be a Christian. You would rather play bridge. Well, then, go to the devil, if that's the way you want to live. I can't stop you.

Whenever I remember I'm a part of the body of Christ, a member of the royal family, I just want to shout "Hallelujah."

In talking to men God must, of course, use the language of men, but He can only put into our words just a little of what He would tell us. A very little looking into the matter, however, will show that He has used the most expressive words in our language to show how near and precious is to be our relationship to Him. In fact, He has used about all the words we have that could be used for that purpose, as members of His body, His bride and sons of God.

If we are so fortunate as to have a part in the meeting in the air, it will mean that we are among the most fortunate of all the sons of men, and that we have lived in the most blessed of all times for men to live, for only those are eligible to membership in the body of Christ who live in the present dispensation.

Moses and David and Isaiah and Jeremiah had no such chance as we have, for the body of Christ had its beginning at Pentecost. Neither will those who live after the rapture have an opportunity, for the body will then be complete and the door closed forever, as it was in the faces of the foolish virgins. Jesus said of John the Baptist that he was the greatest of all prophets, but that the least in the kingdom of God was greater than he.

What an awful thing it would be, then, to have such a glorious opportunity and miss it! Others will know the joys of great salvation, for the world will be saved during the millennium (the next dispensation), and the knowledge of the glory of God will cover the earth as the waters cover the sea, but the people of that day will have no place in the body of Christ; they cannot become members of the royal family. They will be loyal subjects of the king.

That is why Paul could say: "For I reckon that the sufferings of this present time are not worthy to be compared with the glory which shall be revealed in us" (Rom. 8:16).

There is a vast difference between a son of King George

and a subject of Great Britain. The smallest babe of royal blood is greater than the greatest man in the kingdom.

2. If we have a place in that meeting in the air it will mean that we are like Christ, for "when he shall appear we shall be like him, for we shall see him as he is."

The true child of God is always longing to be like his Master, and this heart yearning is the sure prophecy of what we shall then be. It will also mean that we shall nevermore be separated from Him. The devil will never again have power to separate us from Him for a single moment, and wherever He is, there shall we be also. The fact that Jesus is to be here during the millennium would be proof conclusive that we shall be here with Him, even if there were no other Scripture for it.

3. For some that meeting will mean that they reached it without having to pass through death, for it is to be composed of those who have gone before, and those who are still living at that time. Some who are born into this world are never to die, and we may hope to be of that elect number.

The Christian has no business to be looking for death. It is his right to hope to live forever, and instead of expecting to go to the grave, he should be looking for the coming of his Lord and the meeting in the air.

4. It will also mean that we shall then have bodies that will remain young forever. Pains and aches, gray hair, wrinkles and feebleness will never again be known. Listen to this:

"Behold, I show you a mystery; we shall not all sleep (die), but we shall all be changed. In a moment, in the twinkling of an eye, at the last trump, for the trumpet shall sound, and the dead shall be raised incorruptible (no longer subject to age or decay), and we shall be changed (into His likeness)" (1 Cor. 15:51-52).

And it will come in the twinkling of an eye—in a moment—and that moment will be what all time was made for.

In that moment some will give up old age to be young forever. Others will go from beds of pain upon which they may have lain prostrate for years. Others, from the most grinding poverty, will spring to eternal wealth. Some will go from burdens from which they expected no relief save death.

From what tribulations and troubles and afflictions will not that moment be a deliverance, and how the angels will begin to crowd the battlements of heaven upon that glad meeting when they know it is about to come! In a moment! In the twinkling of an eye!

"Come, Lord Jesus; come quickly," ought to be the daily prayer of every Christian heart. And yet as we look about us now, and see how the devil seems to be having his way as much as ever, it looks as if that great time would never come.

But you can't tell by appearances. An hour before the tidal wave comes there is nothing to indicate that it will ever come. Nobody dreamed of an earthquake ten minutes before San Francisco began to rock and rumble.

Some time ago the President touched a golden key in the White House and in a moment, in the twinkling of an eye, the acres of machinery at the great Seattle exposition, on the other side of the country, were in motion, and countless flags began to fly in the breeze; and that's the way the Lord will come.

Just that quick! Quicker than a clock can tick! Quicker than lightning can flash! Ten minutes before the President touched the golden key it looked as if the machinery would never start, but when the right moment arrived it was going.

"Therefore, be ye ready, for in such an hour as ye think not the son of man cometh." God's clock is never behind the smallest fraction of a second.

All signs point to the great event, some of which seemed to me to be:

(a) Radical tendency to depart from the Christian life.
(b) Prophecies fulfilled—the gospel has been preached in every nation.
(c) The worldwide expectancy of His coming.
(d) Revival among the Jews. They are flocking to Jerusalem.
(e) The political unrest.

(f) Extreme views on questions of government.
(g) Concentration of wealth in the hands of the few.

5. If we have a part in that meeting it will mean that we shall be here in this world with the Lord during the millennium—a thousand years—with the devil chained and cast out—not a saloon, gambling hell or brothel in the world, and everything just as we want it. Hear this:

"And cast him into the bottomless pit, and shut him up, and set a seal upon him, that he should deceive the nations no more, till the thousand years should be fulfilled; and after that he must be loose a little season.

"And I saw thrones, and they sat upon them, and judgment was given unto them; and I saw the souls of them that were beheaded for the witness of Jesus, and for the word of God, and which had not worshiped the beast, neither his image, neither had received his mark upon their foreheads, or in their hands, and they lived and reigned with Christ a thousand years.

"But the rest of the dead lived not again until the thousand years were finished. This is the first resurrection.

"Blessed and holy is he that hath part in the first resurrection: on such the second death hath no power, but they shall be priests of God and of Christ, and shall reign with him a thousand years" (Rev. 20:3-6).

6. To have part in this meeting will be to meet those who have gone on before—fathers and mothers and other loved ones. Think of how glorious and blessed that will be, and there will doubtless be infinite surprises that the Lord will have in store for us, "For it hath not entered into the heart of man the things that the Lord hath prepared for them that love him."

7. Think of the delight of meeting and continuing with the other members of the Lord's body, who will then be as dear to us as the apple of our own eye. Think of being intimate with Peter, James and John, Andrew, Philip and the others, and of hearing from them again and again all the incidents they witnessed in the life of Jesus.

Think of being more intimate with Paul and Silas and

Mark and Luke and Timothy, and the saints who were in Caesar's household, than we are with our very best friends now.

Think of knowing Mary, the mother of Jesus, as well as you know your own mother, and of having her intimate friends, Martha and Mary Magdalene, and the unknown disciples who on the first Easter morning walked with their risen Lord on the way to Emmaus!

Think of talking with Zaccheus and Blind Bartimeus, the daughter of Jairus, and the wild man out of whom the legion of devils were cast. And the blind man in the ninth chapter of John—how good it will be to shake hands with him and tell him some of the good things we have so often thought about his courage.

And Joseph of Arimathea, Nicodemus and the boy who had the five loaves and two fishes. And the sick woman who touched the hem of His garment; the widow who gave the two mites and the Philippian jailer who got the old-time religion in an unmistakable way; the first leper who was cleansed, and all the rest. How much we shall miss, if we miss that meeting in the air.

8. Think of how glorious it will be to live for a thousand years in this world with our blessed Master and be closely associated with Him; with bodies that will not wear out or grow old, always in perfect health, and with faculties for enjoyment a thousand times higher than we possess now.

The millennium will be the greatest time ever known, for it will be the golden age of man. Poverty, sickness, war and pestilence will be unknown. There will be no devil to cause human suffering and woe.

Then think of the delight of coming back into this world, where we have had so much trouble and hardship and poverty and sickness, to live under such glorious circumstances as will then prevail.

A man told a friend of mine that when a boy he footed it for nearly a hundred miles over the old National road. It was in August, the weather hot and dusty, and the boy penniless, homeless and disheartened. He had on a pair of cowhide shoes, and his feet became so sore that over much of the way he could only hobble along in great pain.

A little while ago he went over the same road in an elegant automobile, and he never so enjoyed a ride in his life. The weather was fine and he had nothing to do but sit there and drink in the beauty of the day, and think of how much better off he was than when he went limping over the same road, a poor, helpless, sore-footed boy.

Well, it will be something like that with us in the millennium, perhaps, only vastly more glorious when we come back to have a good time here.

9. It will also mean to be richly rewarded for all we have ever done or suffered for the Lord. Near the close of his hard and strenuous life, Paul said:

"Henceforth there is laid up for me a crown of righteousness, which the Lord, the righteous judge, shall give me at that day; and not to me only, but unto all them that love His appearing" (2 Tim. 4:8).

Here are other verses showing there is to be a reward:

"And when the chief shepherd shall appear ye shall receive a crown of glory that fadeth not away" (1 Peter 5:4). "And behold, I come quickly, and my reward is with me to give every man according as his work shall be" (Rev. 22:12).

10. If we have a part in that meeting, we shall escape the great tribulation which is to come upon all the earth as soon as the members of the body of Christ are taken out of the world.

The body of Christ is now the salt of the earth, and the light of the world. It is the army with which God now holds in check the principalities and powers of evil. It is therefore evident that when this army is taken out of the world, the devil will have unhindered sway, and will immediately begin to make this world as much like hell as he wants it to be. In speaking of this awful time, Jesus said:

"Then shall be great tribulation, such as was not since the beginning of the world to this time, no, nor ever shall be. And except those days should be shortened, there shall no flesh be saved; but for the elect's sake those days shall be shortened" (Matt. 24:21-22).

And here is what Daniel says of it:

"And there shall be a time of trouble such as never was since there was a nation even to that time, and at that time thy people shall be delivered (members of the Lord's body), every one that shall be found written in the book" (Dan. 12:1).

Human imagination is incapable of picturing the awfulness of this great tribulation, that is surely coming on the world, and may begin this very day—yes, even this very hour!

Think of it! It is to be the worst time the world has ever known, or ever will know. A worse time than the flood; a worse time than the bondage of Egypt, and a worse time than the destruction of Jerusalem, when women and children were torn in pieces, and the very name of mercy was unknown.

A worse time than the reign of Nero; worse than during the Spanish inquisition; worse than when Cortes destroyed the Aztecs; worse than during the French revolution and the commune, and worse than during the Dark Ages.

A worse time than when men were skinned alive; worse than when they were pulled asunder by horses; worse than when men, women and children were thrown to hungry lions, and worse than when they were dipped in pitch and burned as torches.

Do you want to live in that kind of a time? Well, the only thing that can surely save you from it is to have a part in that meeting in the air, for no others who are living at that time can escape from it, and that awful time may be upon us within the next ten minutes, for it will begin at the very moment the rapture takes place.

There is now not a single prophecy remaining to be fulfilled before the Lord may come, and the members of His body be caught up to meet Him in the air.

It stands to reason that the tribulation must be the most awful time known, because for the only time in all history the devil will then be loose and have unhindered sway.

Everything he can do that will add to human woe will certainly be done. Governments will go to pieces, and there will be no security of life and property. A man may be a millionaire one day, a beggar the next.

A very chaos of crime and outrage of every kind will be turned loose. God will let the world and the universe see for a time what it will mean to live under the devil's rule, and will let those who pass through the tribulation just what is meant by sowing the wind and reaping the whirlwind.

It is supposed that the tribulation will cover a period of seven years. It might be seven hundred years, but it cannot be less than seven years. God in His mercy will make it as short as possible. That the real church of God, believers, members of the body of Christ, are to be taken out of the world before the world is saved is as clearly taught in the Bible as that through the atonement made by Christ man may have salvation from sin.

What will it mean to the world? Every believer will be instantly taken out of the world; homes will be rent in twain, husbands will be robbed of godly wives, children will be taken out of the world and those left behind will wring their hands in grief.

No doubt newspapers will print extra editions. Universal consternation will reign. The world will neither see the Lord, neither will they see their loved ones go. Those who have died in the faith will be raised.

The statement of Jesus shows that not all the people are to be caught up in the air in the clouds, but one here and there:

"There shall be two men in one bed; one shall be taken and the other left. Two women shall be grinding together; the one shall be taken and the other left. Two men shall be in the field; the one shall be taken and the other left" (Luke 17:34-36).

This makes it look as if the number caught up in the air would not be large. When will the meeting in the air occur? In regard to this Jesus said:

"But of that day and hour knoweth no man, no, not the angels which are in heaven—neither the son, but the father. Take ye heed, watch and pray; for ye know not when the time is" (Mark 13:32-33).

But He also said, after speaking of conditions that would prevail about that time:

"So, likewise ye, when ye shall see all these things, know that it is near, even at the doors" (Matt. 24:33).

Will the world come to an end when Jesus comes and takes away the members of His body? No, not for at least 1,000 years; perhaps longer. The millennium must come after Jesus comes, and must have its beginning at the close of the great tribulation.

The real truth is, that great event will not bring destruction to anything that is good, but will, on the contrary, introduce an era of the greatest progress and prosperity the world has ever known.

The coming of Christ will bring the millennium—the golden age of man in this world—when the arts and sciences, and everything else that man ought to delight in, will flourish as never before, and never until Jesus comes will the knowledge of the glory of God cover the earth as the waters cover the sea.

To say that the second coming of Christ is a pernicious thing to preach is the same as saying it would be a calamity for God to rule. It will be the culmination of the redemption of this world, and to say that it would put an end to all progress is as foolish as to say that putting the roof on a house would ruin it and throw the carpenters out of work.

There is nothing more clearly declared in the Bible than that Christ will come and reign on earth during the millennium, when all will be restored that was lost by the fall. Then and only then will God's will be done on earth as it is in heaven.

The scribes and Pharisees thought that business was going to be endangered by Christ's first coming. The only business that will be hurt by the second coming of Christ will be the devil's business. At the time of His coming there will be no general resurrection or judgment.

At the close of the millennium reign of Christ the devil will be loosed out of the pit for a season, and look for the first time upon a world without sin. He will tempt people. They will be as foolish as now and yield to his lies and subtlety.

He will gather his hosts and come against the saints to battle. Fire will fall from heaven and consume them. Then takes place the resurrection of the wicked dead. Then the judgment of the great white throne, with Christ to judge.

There is this about it, however: We are living nearer to it than anybody ever lived before, and when it does come it is going to come in a moment—in the twinkling of an eye—and the only safe course for us to pursue is to be ready for the bridegroom when He comes.

"Take ye heed, watch and pray, for ye know not when the time is. For the son of man is as a man taking a far journey, who left his house and gave authority to his servants, and to every man his work, and commanded the porter to watch" (Mark 13:33-36).

We are not told when Jesus will come, but we are told that His coming is sure, and we are charged to watch for it. How it would affect our lives and make hard things easy to bear if we would only do this and always be doing this.

Don't you know how eagerly you get ready for company that you love when you receive a telegram saying that they are surely coming? How you clean house and want to have everything in the very best kind of order!

If we were continually looking for the coming of Jesus we would be as careful to keep our lives as clean as you would be to have your homes clean if you were expecting company. The certainty of His coming would also be a constant source of comfort and inspiration to us, if we believed it to be near.

The Lord does not come to the world at the time of the rapture, but only reveals Himself to the members of His body. At the time of His resurrection He was only seen by those who believed on Him. Pilate and the high priest, and those who crucified Him, did not know that He was risen. So it will be at the time of the rapture. The world will not know that He has been here, and will have no knowledge of Him until He comes with the members of His body, at the close of the tribulation.

What an awful thing, then, to have the glorious privilege of living in His dispensation, with all it means, and miss getting into the body of Christ by refusing to become a Christian.

The preacher owes it to his people to look into these things, that he may show them their great privilege, and warn them of the awful things that may come upon them, if they miss their chance and have to go through the great tribulation. The preacher who has never qualified himself to preach a sermon on the sure and certain coming of his Master will have to answer for an awful breach of trust when he stands before Him.

Our fleet of battleships made its remarkable trip around the Horn and around the world, and again dropped anchor at home on schedule time, almost to the minute, in spite of storm and the fickleness of the wind and wave, and if the calculations of men can be wrought out so precisely, certainly we have the right to expect that God will execute His plans with absolute precision in whatever task He sets for Himself.

Certainly we can think of nothing so improbable as that He would complete His program for creation on schedule time, and yet would so tie His own hands by failure to anticipate and provide for all possible emergencies and contingencies that the train of His purpose for redemption would be so delayed or nearly wrecked that it would almost have to be abandoned.

Do not think it for a moment. God's purpose can no more be kept back a minute than the heavenly bodies can be delayed a minute. In redemption God is working by the clock as surely as in creation, and His chariot of salvation is not marked late by a single minute.

Come, Lord Jesus!

# NOTES

## "The Marriage of the Lamb"

**Charles Haddon Spurgeon** (1834-1892) is undoubtedly the most famous minister of modern times. Converted in 1850, he united with the Baptists and soon began to preach in various places. He became pastor of the Baptist church in Waterbeach in 1851, and three years later he was called to the decaying Park Street Church, London. Within a short time, the work began to prosper, a new church was built and dedicated in 1861, and Spurgeon became London's most popular preacher. In 1855, he began to publish his sermons weekly; and today they make up the fifty-seven volumes of *The Metropolitan Pulpit.* He founded a pastor's college and several orphanages.

This sermon is taken from *The Metropolitan Tabernacle Pulpit*, volume 35, and was preached on Sunday morning, July 21, 1889.

**Charles Haddon Spurgeon**

# 2

# "THE MARRIAGE OF THE LAMB"

LET US BE GLAD and rejoice, and give honor to him: for the marriage of the Lamb is come, and his wife hath made herself ready. And to her was granted that she should be arrayed in fine linen, clean and white: for the fine linen is the righteousness of saints (Revelation 19:7,8).

Last Lord's day we saw clearly from God's Word that our Lord is worshiped in heaven under the character of a Lamb. Now, by a Lamb was meant sacrifice, sacrifice for the putting away of sin: according to the text, "Behold the Lamb of God, which taketh away the sin of the world." It is against the great doctrine of atonement and substitutionary death that the attacks of the present unbelieving age are constantly being made; and therefore, I set before you the truth that substitution and sacrifice were not a temporary expedient, but that they continue all through the whole history of salvation, and remain in the very highest place, even in heaven itself, and will continue evermore. Do not forget that, whenever we read of Christ as a Lamb, it is to remind us of His sufferings and death in our room, and place, and stead, for the putting away of our sin. Under that character we looked to Him, some of us, years ago, and found peace at the first. We are still looking to Him under that same character; and when we attain to heaven, we shall not have to change our thought of Him, but we shall still see Him as a Lamb that has been slain. In our lowest place, when we came out of the Egypt of our bondage, He was the Lamb of God's passover; and in our highest place, in the heavenly temple, we shall still regard Him as "the Lamb slain from the foundation of the world."

This morning my principal aim shall be to show you that the blessed and glorious union, which is to be celebrated between the church and her Lord, will be the marriage *"of the Lamb."* The ever blessed and eternal union of hearts with Christ will be in reference to His sacrifice, specially and emphatically. The perfected union of the entire church of God with her divine Husband is here described by the beloved apostle, who laid his head upon his Master's bosom, and knew most about Him, and who was under the immediate inspiration of the Holy Spirit, in these words: "The marriage of the Lamb is come, and his wife hath made herself ready."

Whatever else we think of at this time, my discourse will aim at this as the white of the target—namely, that Jesus Christ as the Lamb, the sacrifice, is not only the beginning, but the end; not only the foundation, but the topstone of the whole sacred edifice of the temple of grace. The consummation of the whole work of redemption is the marriage of the church to Christ; and, according to "the true sayings of God," this is "the marriage of the Lamb."

I will set forth this marriage as best I am able. It is divinely veiled as well as revealed in this Revelation. God forbid we should intrude where the Holy Sprit shuts us out; but still, what we do know of it, let us now think upon, and may the sacred Spirit make it profitable to us!

## The Antecedents of This Marriage

I. First, I invite your attention to the antecedents of this marriage. What will happen before the public marriage is celebrated?

One great event will be *the destruction of the harlot church*. I have just read, in your hearing, the previous chapter, which declares the overwhelming destruction which will fall upon that evil system. Any church which puts in the place of justification by faith in Christ another method of salvation, is a harlot church. The doctrine of justification by faith in Christ is the article of a standing or a falling church. Where the blood is precious, there is life; where atonement by the sacrifice is preached and loved, there will the Spirit of God bear effectual testimony; but where human priests are put in the place of Jesus, where pardons can be purchased, where there is an unbloody sacrifice instead of the great propitiation, and sacraments are exalted as the means of regeneration; there the church is no longer a chaste virgin unto Christ, but she hath turned aside from her purity.

The Antichristian system is to be utterly extirpated and burnt with fire; for you will perceive, in the fourteenth verse the seventeenth chapter, that those who were associated with this false church, "shall make war with the Lamb, and the Lamb shall overcome them: for He is Lord of lords, and King of kings"; and there has been no more wicked nor more determined war with the Lamb than that which has been waged by superstition supported by unbelief. The harlot church and the beast of infidelity are in real league against the simple faith of Christ. If you point men, no matter where—if you point them away from Christ, you point them to Antichrist. If you teach them what you may, no matter how philosophical it may seem—if in any way it takes them off from building upon the one foundation of Christ's glorious and finished work, you have laid an Antichristian foundation, and all that is built thereon will be destroyed. Everything which sets up itself in opposition to the sacrifice of Christ, is to be hurled down, and made to sink like a millstone in the flood. I would God the hour were come! Oh, that the Lord's own right arm were bare, and that we heard the cry, "Babylon the great is fallen, is fallen." It is ours to expect the speedy coming of our Lord; yet, if He tarry, it may be many a day before "her plagues come in one day." But, wait as we may, so it shall be; the day must come when the true church shall be honored, and the harlot church shall be abhorred. The Bride of Christ is a sort of Cinderella now, sitting among the ashes. She is like her Lord, "despised and rejected of men"; the watchmen smite her, and take away her veil from her; for they know her not, even as they knew not her Lord. But when He shall appear, then shall she appear also, and in His glorious manifestation she also shall shine forth as the sun in the kingdom of the Father.

Furthermore, in the immediate connection, we note that before the marriage of the Lamb, *there was a peculiar voice*. Read the fifth verse: "And a voice came." Where from? "A voice came out of the throne." Whose voice was that? It was not the voice of the Eternal God; for it said, "Praise our God, all ye his servants." Whose voice, then, could it be? No one but God could be upon the throne save the Lamb, who is God. Surely, it was He who said, "Praise our God." The Mediator, God-and-man in one person, was on the throne as a Lamb, and He announced the day of His own marriage. Who should do it but He? "A voice came out of the throne, saying, Praise our God, all ye his servants, and ye that fear him, both small and great." He speaks the word which calls on all the servants of God to praise Him, because His complete victory had come. Longing to see of the travail of His soul, earnest to gather in all His elect, He speaks; for the fullness of time has come, when His joy shall be full, and He shall rejoice over the whole company of His redeemed as forever one with Himself.

*The voice from the throne is a very remarkable one*; for it shows how near akin the exalted Christ is to His people. He saith to all the redeemed, "Praise *our* God, all ye his servants." It reminds me of His memorable words, "I ascend unto my Father, and your Father; and to my God, and your God." He was not then ashamed to associate His people with Him in the high possession of His Father and His God; and up there upon the throne, He saith, "Praise *our* God." I do not know how this language strikes you; but to me it forcibly sets forth His love, His condescension, His fraternization, His union with His people. Since I know not how to set it out to you, I must leave you to think over it. He who has gone triumphantly up to the throne, the Savior whose conflicts are all over, who has gained the everlasting reward of sitting with the Father upon His throne, still joins with us in praise, and saith, "Praise *our* God, all ye his servants." He is not even ashamed to have fellowship with the least of His people; for He adds, "And ye that fear him, both small and great." Truly "the man is near of kin to us, he is our next kinsman."

In ties of blood, with sinners one,
Our Jesus hath to glory gone.

In that glory He still owns His dear relationship, and in the midst of the church He singeth praise unto God (Heb. 2:11,12).

Next, notice *the response to this voice*; for this also precedes the marriage. No sooner did that one august voice summon them to praise, then immediately "I heard as it were the voice of a great multitude." He heard the mingled sound as of an innumerable host all joining in the song; for the redeemed of the Lord are not a few. No man can count them. "Out of every kindred, and tongue, and people, and nation," they respond in that day to the voice of the Lamb, saying, "Alleluia: for the Lord God omnipotent reigneth." So loud was the sound of all those commingled voices, that it sounded like "many waters"; like cataracts in their roar, or like oceans in their fullness. It was as though all the billows of the Atlantic, and the Pacific, and the Northern, and the Southern oceans lifted up their voices, and deep answered unto deep.

Nor was the figure too strong; for John heaps upon it another comparison, and says, "As the voice of mighty thunderings." We have lately heard the thunder above the deafening din of our streets, and we have trembled at the dread artillery of heaven. Such was the sound of the mingled voices of the redeemed when they all united to give honor to God, because the marriage of the Lamb had come. Who can imagine the acclamations of that glorious day? We now preach the gospel, as it were, in a corner, and few there are that will applaud the King of kings. Still, the Christ wendeth His way through the world as an unknown or forgotten man; and His church, following behind Him, seemeth as a forlorn and forsaken woman—few there be that care for her. But in that day when her Lord is seen as the King of kings, and she is openly acknowledged as His spouse, what welcomes will be heard, what bursts of adoring praise unto the Lord God omnipotent!

Observe that *this tremendous volume of sound will be full of rejoicing and of devout homage.* "Let us be glad and rejoice, and give honor to Him." Double joy will be there, and its expression will be homage to the Lord God. The joy of joys will be the delight of Christ in His perfectly gathered church. There is joy in heaven in the presence of the angels of God over one sinner that repenteth; but when all these repenting sinners are gathered into one perfected body, and married to the Lamb, what will be the infinite gladness? Heaven is always heaven, and unspeakably full of blessedness; but even heaven has its holidays, even bliss has its overflowings; and on that day when the springtide of the infinite ocean of joy shall have come, what a measureless flood of delight shall overflow the souls of all glorified spirits as they perceive that the consummation of love's great design is come—"The marriage of the Lamb is come, and his wife hath made herself ready!" We do not know yet, beloved, of what happiness we are capable. We have sometimes wished that we could

> "Sit and sing ourselves away
> To everlasting bliss."

But then we were only feeling the spray of the ocean of blessedness. What must it be to bathe in it? Here we drink from cups of consolation; but what draughts we shall have when we lie down at the well-head, and drink in our joy immediately from God! If you and I enter glory soon without our bodies, we shall not even then know to the utmost degree what will be the bliss of our perfected manhood, when the body shall be raised incorruptible from among the dead, and joined to the sinless soul. Nor would this give us more than a bare idea of the infinite blessedness of myriads of such perfected manhoods united in a perfected church; from which no one single member shall be missing, nor one member maimed, or sick, or stained. Praise the Lord Jesus as you sing:

> Thou the whole body shalt present
> Before thy Father's face;
> Nor shall a wrinkle, or a spot,
> The beauteous form deface.

Oh, what joy! I feel as if I could not preach to you: I want to get away to think it over, and chew the cud of meditation for myself. You must just sit where you are and muse. Here we have the essence of heavenly music in a few plain words. "The marriage of the Lamb is come." Oh, may I be there! May I be a part of the perfected body of the church of God! Oh, that I might be but part of the soles of her feet, or the least hair of her head! If I may but see the King in His beauty, in the fullness of His joy, when He shall take by the right hand her for whom He shed His precious blood, and shall know the joy which was set before Him, for which He endured the cross, despising the shame, I shall be blest indeed!

Thus, I have given you a hint of what will precede the marriage of the Lamb, in all of which you may observe that Jesus wears His character of the Lamb. The harlot church hath fought against the Lamb, and the Lamb hath overcome her forces. He it is that, on the throne, speaks to His people as His brethren; it is to Him that the response is given; for the joy and the delight all spring from the fact that the marriage is that of the Lamb whom the Father glorifies, and who glorifies the Father. The voice said, "Let us rejoice, and give honor to him." Was not that His prayer of old, "Father, glorify thy Son, that thy Son also may glorify thee"? To glorify the Father, Jesus died as a sacrifice; and to glorify Jesus, the Father gives Him His church, which is redeemed by the blood of the Lamb.

## The Marriage Itself

II. Now may I be helped by the Spirit of God, while I lead you on to the marriage itself. "The marriage of the Lamb is come." Often as you hear about this marriage of the Lamb, I greatly question whether any here have any precise idea what it means. Dean Alford says, "This figure of a marriage between the Lord and his people, is too frequent and familiar to need explanation." With all deference to the excellent divine, that was a very sufficient reason why He should have carefully explained it, since that which is often noted in Holy Scripture must be of first importance, and should be well understood. I do not wonder that many are shy of such a theme, for it is a difficult one. Alas, how little do I, personally, know of such a matter!

The marriage of the Lamb is *the result of the eternal*

*gift of the Father.* Our Lord says, "Thine they were, and thou gavest them me." His prayer was, "Father, I will that they also, whom thou hast given me, be with me where I am; that they may behold my glory, which thou hast given me: for thou lovedst me before the foundation of the world." The Father made a choice, and the chosen He gave to His Son to be His portion. For them He entered into a covenant of redemption, whereby He was pledged in due time to take upon Himself their nature, pay the penalty of their offenses, and set them free to be His own. Beloved, that which was arranged in the councils of eternity and settle there between the high contracting parties, is brought to its ultimate end in that day when the Lamb takes unto Himself in everlasting union the whole of those whom His Father gave Him from of old.

Next: this is *the completion of the betrothal,* which took place with each of them in time. I shall not attempt elaborate distinctions; but as far as you and I were concerned, the Lord Jesus betrothed each one of us unto Himself in righteousness, when first we believed on Him. Then He took us to be His, and gave Himself to be ours, so that we could sing—"My beloved is mine, and I am His." This was the essence of the marriage. Paul, in the Epistle of the Ephesians, represents our Lord as already married to the church. This may be illustrated by the Oriental custom, by which, when the bride is betrothed, all the sanctities of marriage are involved in those espousals; but yet there may be a considerable interval before the bride is taken to her husband's house. She dwells with her former household, and has not yet forgotten her kindred and her father's house, though still she is espoused in truth and righteousness. Afterwards, she is brought home on an appointed day, the day which we should call the actual marriage; but yet the betrothal is, to Orientals, of the very essence of the marriage. Well, then, you and I are betrothed to our Lord today, and He is joined to us by inseparable bonds. He does not wish to part with us, nor could we part from Him. He is the delight of our souls, and He rejoices over us with singing. Rejoice that He has chosen you and called you, and through the betrothal look forward to the marriage. Feel even now, that though in the world, you are not of it: your destiny does not lie here among these frivolous sons of men. Our home is henceforth on high.

> My heart is with him on his throne,
> And ill can brook delay;
> Each moment listening for the voice,
> "Rise up, and come away."

*The marriage day indicates the perfecting of the body of the church.* I have already told you that the church will then be completed, and it is not so now. Adam lay asleep, and the Lord took out of his side a rib, and fashioned thereof a help-meet for him: Adam saw her not when she was in the forming, but he opened his eyes, and before him was the perfect form of his help-meet. Beloved, the true church is now in the forming, and is therefore not visible. There are many churches; but as to the one church of Christ, we see it neither here nor there. We speak of the visible church; but the term is not correct. The thing which we see is a mixture of believers and mere pretenders to faith. The church which is affianced unto the heavenly Bridegroom is not visible as yet; for she is in the process of formation. The Lord will not allow such simpletons as we are to see His half-finished work. But the day will come when He shall have completed His new creation, and then will He bring her forth whom He has made for the second Adam, to be His delight to all eternity. The church is not perfected as yet. We read of that part of it which is in heaven, that "They without us should not be made perfect." Unless you and I get there, if we are true believers, there cannot be a perfect church in glory. The music of the heavenly harmonies as yet lacks certain voices. Some of its needful notes are too bass for those already, and others are too high for them, till the singers come who are ordained to give the choir its fullest range. At the Crystal Palace you have seen the singers come trooping in. The conductor is all anxiety if they seem to linger. Still, some are away. The time is nearly up, and you see seats up there on the right, and a vacant block down there on the left. Even so with the heavenly harmony. Beloved, in the day of the marriage of the Lamb, the chosen shall all be there—the great and the small—even all the believers who are wrestling hard this day with sins and doubts and fears. Every living member of the living church shall be there to be married to the Lamb.

By this marriage is meant more than I have told you. There is the *home-bringing*. You are not to live here forever in these tents of Kedar, among a people of a strange tongue; but the blessed Bridegroom cometh to take you to the happy country, where you shall no longer say, "My soul is among lions." All the faithful shall soon be away to thy land, O Emmanuel! We shall dwell in the land that floweth with milk and honey, the land of the unclouded and unsetting sun, the home of the blessed of the Lord. Happy indeed will be the home-bringing of the perfect church!

The marriage is the *coronal-avowal*. The church is the bride of the great King, and He will set the crown upon her head, and make her to be known as His true spouse forever. Oh, what a day that will be when every member of Christ shall be crowned in Him, and with Him, and every member of the mystical body shall be glorified in the glory of the Bridegroom! Oh, may I be there in that day! Brethren, we must be with our Lord in the fight if we would be with Him in the victory. We must be with Him in wearing the crown of thorns, if we are to be with Him in wearing the crown of glory. We must be faithful by His grace, even unto death, if we are to share the glory of His endless life.

I cannot tell you all it means, but certainly this marriage signifies that all who have believed in Him shall then *enter into a bliss which shall never end*; a bliss which no fear approacheth, or doubt becloudeth. They shall be forever with the Lord, forever glorified with Him. Expect not lips of clay fitly to speak on such a theme. Tongues of fire are needed, and words that fall like fire-flakes on the soul.

A day will come, the day of days, time's crown and

glory, when, all conflict, risk, and judgment ended forever, the saints, arrayed in the righteousness of Christ, shall be eternally one with Him in living, loving, lasting union, partaking together of the same glory, the glory of the Most High. What must it be to be there! My dear hearers, will you be there? Make your calling and election sure. If you are not trusting the Lamb on earth, you will not reign with the Lamb in His glory. He that doth not love the Lamb, as the atoning sacrifice, shall never be the bride of the Lamb. How can you hope to be glorified with Him if you neglect Him in the day of His scorning? O Lamb of God, my sacrifice, I must be one with thee, for this is my very life! I could not live apart from thee. If, my hearer, thou canst thus speak, there is good hope that thou shalt be a participator in the marriage of the Lamb.

## The Character Under Which the Bridegroom Appears Is That of the Lamb

III. But we pass on now to dwell emphatically upon the fact that the character under which the Bridegroom appears is that of the Lamb. "The marriage of *the Lamb* is come."

It must be so, because first of all *our Savior was the Lamb in the eternal covenant*; when this whole matter was planned, arranged, and settled by the foresight and decree of eternity. He is "the Lamb slain from the foundation of the world," and the covenant was with Him, as one who was to be the surety, the substitute, the sacrifice for guilty men. So, and not otherwise, was it of old.

It was next *as the Lamb that He loved us and proved His love*. Beloved, He did not give us words of love merely when He came from heaven to earth, and dwelt among us "a lowly man before his foes"; but He proceeded to deeds of truest affection. The supreme proof of His love was that He was led as a lamb to the slaughter. When He poured out His blood as a sacrifice, it might have been said, "Behold, how he loved them!" If you would prove the love of Jesus, you would not mention the transfiguration, but the crucifixion. Gethsemane and Golgotha would rise to your lips. Here to demonstration, beyond all possibility of doubt by any true heart, the Well-beloved proved His love to us. See how it runs: "He loved me, and gave Himself for me," as if that giving of Himself for me was the clear proof that He loved me. Read again: "Christ loved the church, and gave Himself for it." The proof of His love to the church was the giving up of Himself for it. "Being found in fashion as a man he humbled himself, and became obedient to death, even the death of the cross." "Herein is love, not that we loved God, but that he loved us." So, you see, as a Lamb He proved His love, and as a Lamb He celebrated His marriage with us.

Go a step further. Love in marriage must be on both sides, and *it is as the Lamb that we first came to love Him*. I had no love to Christ, how could I have, till I saw His wounds and blood? "We love him, because he first loved us." His perfect life was a condemnation to me, much as I was compelled to admire it; but the love that drew me to Him was shown in His substitutionary character, when He bore my sins in His own body on the tree. Is it not so with you, beloved? I have heard a great deal about conversions through admiration of the character of Christ, but I have never met with one: all I have ever met with have been conversions through a sense of need of salvation, and a consciousness of guilt, which could never be satisfied save by His agony and death, through which sin is justly pardoned, and evil is subdued. This is the great heart-winning doctrine. Christ loves us as the Lamb, and we love Him as the Lamb.

Further, *marriage is the most perfect union*. Surely, it is as the Lamb that Jesus is most closely joined to His people. Our Lord came very close to us when He took our nature, for thus He became bone of our bone, and flesh of our flesh. He came very near to us when, for this cause, He left His Father and became one flesh with His church. He could not be sinful as she was; but He did take her sins upon Himself, and bear them all away, as it is written, "The Lord hath laid on Him the iniquity of us all." When "he was numbered with the transgressors," and when the sword of vengeance smote Him in our stead, then He came nearer to us than ever He could do in the perfection of His Incarnation. I cannot conceive of closer union than that of Christ and souls redeemed by blood. As I look at Him in death, I feel forced to cry, "Surely a husband by blood art thou to me, O Jesus! Thou art joined to me by something closer than the one fact that thou art of my nature; for that nature of thine has borne my sin, and suffered the penalty of wrath on my behalf. Now art thou one with me in all things, by a union like to that which links thee with the Father." A wonderful union is thus effected by our Lord's wearing the character of the Lamb.

Once more, *we never feel so one with Jesus as when we see Him as the Lamb*. I shall again appeal to your experience. When have you had the sweetest fellowship with Christ in all your lives? I answer on my own account—it has been when I have sung:

> Oh, how sweet to view the flowing
> Of his soul-redeeming blood,
> With divine assurance knowing
> He hath made my peace with God!

If I had my choice today, while abiding in this present state, to see my Lord in His glory, or on His cross, I should choose the latter. Of course, I would prefer to see His glory, and be away with Him; but, while dwelling here surrounded with sin and sorrow, a sight of His griefs has the most effect upon me. "O sacred head once wounded," I long to behold Thee! I never feel so close to my Lord as when I survey His wondrous cross, and see Him pouring out His blood for me. I have been melted down when we have sung together those sweet lines:

> See from his head, his hands, his feet,
> Sorrow and love flow mingled down!
> Did e'er such love and sorrow meet?
> Or thorns compose so rich a crown?

I have almost felt myself in His arms, and like John, I have leaned on His bosom, when I have beheld His passion. I do not wonder, therefore, that since He comes closest to us as the Lamb, and since we come closest to Him when we behold Him in that character, He is pleased to call His highest eternal union with His church, "the marriage of the Lamb."

And O beloved, when you come to think of it, to be married to Him, to be one with Him, to have no thought, no object, no desire, no glory but that which dwells in Him that liveth and was dead—will not this be heaven indeed, where the Lamb is the light thereof? Forever to contemplate and adore Him who offered up Himself without spot unto God, as our sacrifice and propitiation; this shall be an endless feast of grateful love. We shall never weary of this subject. If you see the Lord coming from Edom, with dyed garments from Bozrah, from the winepress wherein He has trampled on His foes, you are overawed and overcome by the terror of that dread display of justice; but when you see Him clad in a vesture dipped in no blood but His own, you will sing aloud evermore, "Thou wast slain, and hast redeemed us to God by thy blood; to thee be glory forever and ever." I could go on singing, "Worthy is Lamb that was slain" throughout all eternity. The theme has an inexhaustible interest about it: there is everything in it: justice, mercy, power, patience, love, condescension, grace and glory. All over glorious is my Lord when I behold Him as a Lamb; and this shall make heaven seven times heaven to me to think that even then I shall be joined to Him in everlasting bonds as the Lamb. [Here a voice from the gallery cried, "Praise the Lord!"] Yes, my friend, we will praise the Lord. "Praise ye the Lord" is the command which was heard coming out of the throne—"Praise our God, all ye his servants, and ye that fear him, both small and great: for the marriage of the Lamb is come, and His wife hath made herself ready."

## The Preparedness of the Bride

IV. Now we come to the last point, the preparedness of the bride: "His wife hath made herself ready." Up till now the church has always been spoken of as His bride, now she is "his wife"—that is a deeper, dearer, more-matured word than "bride": "*his wife* hath made herself ready." The church has now come to the fullness of her joy, and has taken possession of her status and dower as "his wife." What does it mean—"hath made herself ready?"

It signifies, first, *she willingly and of her own accord comes to her Lord,* to be His, and be with Him forever. This she does with all her heart: "she hath made herself ready." She does not enter into this engagement with reluctance. Some unwisely speak of the grace of God, as though it were a physical force, which sets a constraint upon the will of the quickened man. Beloved, I never preach to you in that fashion. Free will is an unknown thing, except it be wrought in us by grace. Grace is the great liberating force. The will is a slave to evil, till grace comes, and makes it free to choose that which is good. No action of the soul is more free than that by which it quits sin, and closes with Christ. Then the man comes to himself. The heart is free from compulsion, when its love goes forth toward the Lord Jesus. I ask you that love Him, do you feel that you are going against your will in so doing? Far from it: you wish to love Him more. In the ultimate union of all the chosen with Christ, will you want any forcing to take your part in the marriage of the Lamb? Did not the words I used just now state your longings—"My heart is with him on his throne." Are you not panting to behold His face? Compulsion to a hungry man to eat would seem more likely than compulsion to be joined unto Christ. His wife hath made herself ready: free grace has made her freely choose Him.

Does it not mean that *she has put away from herself all evil,* and all connection with the corruptions of the harlot church has been destroyed? She has struggled against error, she has fought against infidelity, and both have been put down by her holy watchfulness and earnest testimony; and so she is ready for her Lord.

Does it not also mean that in the great day of the consummation *the church will be one*? Alas, for the divisions among us! You do not know what denomination my friend belonged to who prayed just now. Well, I shall not tell you. You could not judge from his prayer. "The saints in prayer appear as one." Denomination! A plague upon denominationalism! There should be but one denomination: we should be denominated by the name of Christ, as the wife is named by her husband's name. As long as the church of Christ has to say, "My right arm is Episcopalian, and my left arm is Wesleyan, and my right foot is Baptist, and my left foot is Presbyterian or Congregational," she is not ready for the marriage. She will be ready when she has washed out these stains, when all her members have "one Lord, one faith, one baptism." Unity is a main part of the readiness here spoken of.

I beg you to notice what *the preparation* was. It is described in the eighth verse: "To her was granted." I will go on further. Whatever preparation it was that she made, in whatever apparel she was arrayed, it was granted to her. Observe that the harlot church wore fine linen also, but then she had with it purple, silk, and scarlet, and precious stones, and pearls. I do not know whence the harlot obtained her apparel, but I know where the true church found her wedding dress, for it is written, "to her was granted." This was a gift of sovereign grace, the free gift of her own Beloved: "To her was granted." She had a grant from the throne, a royal grant. We have nothing of our own to carry us there by right, nothing of boasted merit; but to us also is granted acceptance in the Beloved. Oh, it is a glorious thing to hold your own by letters patent, under the Great Seal of heaven! When we shall be united to Jesus, the ever blessed Lamb, in endless wedlock, all our fitness to be there will be ours by free grant.

Look at the apparel of the wife, "To her was granted that she should be arrayed in fine linen, clean and white." How simple her raiment! Only fine linen, clean and white. The more simple our worship, the better. The true church of Christ is content with white linen, and no more. She asked not for those fine things we read about in connection with the harlot. She envied not the unchaste one her harpers, and musicians, and pipers, and trumpeters: she was content with her simple harp and joyful song. She did not need all manner of vessels of ivory, and precious wood, brass and iron, and marble. She did not seek for cinnamon, and odors, and ointments, nor aught else of that finery with which people nowadays try to adorn their worship. The simpler the better. When in worship you cannot hear the voices of the people beyond the noise which might be made by the twitter of half-a-dozen sparrows, because a flood of noise from a huge organ is drowning all the praise—I think we have lost our way. The simpler the worship the better, whether in prayer or praise, or anything else. The harlot church bedecks herself with her architecture, and her millinery, and her perfumery, and her oratory, and her music; but those who would follow the Lamb whithersoever He goeth, will keep their worship, their practice, and their doctrine pure and simple, avoiding all the blandishments of carnal policy and human wisdom, content with the truth as it is in Jesus. What more beautiful than pure white linen?

In the Greek, our text runs thus: "Fine linen, clean and white, for fine linen is *the righteousness of the saints.*" Our Revised Version has, in this case, not given us a translation, but an explanation, and that explanation is a contraction of the sense. The revisers word it, "Fine linen is the righteous acts of saints." That word "acts" is of their own insertion. The word "righteousness" has a fuller meaning: it is exceeding broad, and they have narrowed it, and misapplied it. We shall have a complete array of righteousness in Christ's righteousness, active and passive—a garment for the head, and a garment for the feet, and for the loins. What righteousness we have! Righteousness imparted by the power of the Spirit; righteousness imputed by the decree of God. Every form of righteousness will go to make up the believer's outfit; only, all of it is *granted*, and none of it is of our own purchasing. We shall not have Christ's righteousness to cover up our sin, as some blasphemously say—for we shall have no sin to cover. We shall not want Christ's righteousness to make an evil heart seem pure: we shall be as perfect as our Father in heaven is perfect. Washed in the blood of the Lamb, we shall have no spot upon us or within us. We shall have a complete righteousness; and in this arrayed, we shall be covered with the beauty of holiness. This garment is most befitting, for it is "The righteousness of saints." Saints ought to have righteousness. They are themselves made holy, and therefore, they ought to be adorned in visible holiness; and so they shall be.

Best of all we shall be arrayed in that day with *that which pleases the Bridegroom*. Do I not remember how He said, "I counsel thee to buy of me white raiment"? Yes, she has remembered His bidding. She has nothing else but that "fine linen" which is the "The righteousness of saints"; and this He delights in. She comes to the Lamb, bearing about her the result of His own passion, and of His own Spirit, and she is well pleasing in His eyes. The Lord sees in her of the travail of His soul, and He is satisfied.

I have done when I have again put this question: Do you trust the Lamb? I warn you, if you have a religion which has no blood of Christ in it, it is not worth a thought: you had better be rid of it, it will be of no use to you. I warn you, also, that unless you love the Lamb you cannot be married to the Lamb; for He will never be married to those who have no love to Him. You must take Jesus as a sacrifice, or not at all. It is useless to say, "I will follow Christ's example." You will not do anything of the sort. It is idle to say, "He shall be my teacher." He will not own you for a disciple unless you will own Him as a sacrifice. You must take Him as the Lamb, or have done with Him. If you do despite to the blood of Christ, you do despite to the whole person of Christ. Christ is nothing to you if He is not your atonement. As many of you as hope to be saved by the works of the law, or by anything else apart from His blood and righteousness, you have un-Christianized yourselves; you have no part in Jesus here, and you shall have no part in Him hereafter, when He shall take to Himself His own redeemed church, to be His spouse forever and ever. God bless you, for Christ's sake. Amen.

# NOTES

## The Two "Comes"

**Charles Haddon Spurgeon** (1834-1892) is undoubtedly the most famous minister of modern times. Converted in 1850, he united with the Baptists and soon began to preach in various places. He became pastor of the Baptist church in Waterbeach in 1851, and three years later he was called to the decaying Park Street Church, London. Within a short time, the work began to prosper, a new church was built and dedicated in 1861, and Spurgeon became London's most popular preacher. In 1855, he began to publish his sermons weekly; and today they make up the fifty-seven volumes of *The Metropolitan Tabernacle Pulpit*. He founded a pastor's college and several orphanages.

This sermon is taken from *The Metropolitan Tabernacle Pulpit*, volume 23, published in 1877, and was preached on December 31, 1876.

**Charles Haddon Spurgeon**

# 3

## THE TWO "COMES"

> And the Spirit and the bride say, Come. And let him that heareth say, Come. And let him that is athirst come. And whosoever will, let him take the water of life freely (Revelation 20:17).

OUR TEXT STANDS at the end of the Book even as this day stands at the end of the year: and it is full of gospel even as we would make our closing Sabbath discourse. It would seem as if the Holy Spirit were loath to put down the pen while so many remained unbelieving, notwithstanding the testimony of the inspired Word, and therefore, ere He closes the canon of Holy Scripture and guards it against all addition or mutilation with most solemn words, He gives one more full, free, earnest, gracious invitation to thirsty souls to come to Christ and drink. So on this last page of the year I would fain write another gospel invitation that those who have not hitherto believed our report may, even on this day of the feast, incline their ear and accept the message of salvation. Ere yet the midnight bell proclaims the birth of a new year, may you be born to God: at any rate once more shall the truth by which men are regenerated be lovingly brought under your attention. I ask those of you who have the Master's ear to put up this request to Him just now, that if the arrows have missed the mark on the previous fifty-two Sabbaths, they may strike the target this time, being directed by the divine Spirit. Pray also that if some have kept the door of their hearts fast closed against the Lord Jesus till now, He may Himself come in the preaching of the Word this morning, and put in His hand by the hole of the door, that their hearts may be moved for Him. In answer to that prayer we shall be sure to get a blessing. Let us expect it and act upon the expectation, and we shall see men flying to Jesus as a cloud, and as doves to their windows.

Are not the words of our text the words of the Lord Jesus? Can they be regarded as the words of John? I think not, for they follow so closely upon the undoubted language of Jesus in the former verse. Thus runs the passage: "I Jesus have sent mine angel to testify unto you these things in the churches. I am the root and the offspring of David, and the bright and morning star. And the Spirit and the bride say, Come." We can hardly, I think, divide the paragraph, and we must, it seems to me, regard our text as the words of the risen Jesus, that morning star whose cheering beams foretell the glorious day. The lover of men's souls had not quite done speaking to sinners; there was a little more to say, and here He says it. The divine Redeemer, leaning from His throne whereon He sits as the reward of His accomplished work, and bending over sinners with the same love which led Him to die for them says, "Let him that heareth say, Come. And let him that is athirst come. And whosoever will, let him take the water of life freely."

Looking at the words, therefore, in that golden light as coming from the dear lips of the Well-beloved, let us notice first, *the heavenward cry of prayer*—"The Spirit and the bride say, Come. And let him that heareth say, Come." These voices go upward to Christ. Then, secondly, let us hear *the earthward cry of invitation*—"Let him that is athirst come. And whosoever will, let him take the water of life freely"; that cry goes outward and downward toward needy and sorrowing spirits. Then, thirdly, we shall pause awhile to notice *the relation between these two cries*; for the coming of Christ is connected with the coming of sinners: and then, as best we can, we shall *observe and expect the response to the two cries*; both from Him who sitteth in the heavens and from souls thirsting here below. O divine Spirit, bless thou the Word.

### The Heavenward Cry of Prayer

I. First, then, our text begins with the heavenward cry of prayer, *"The Spirit and the bride say, Come. And let him that heareth say, Come."* I think it will be evident, if you read carefully, that this cannot be interpreted as being only the voice of the Spirit and the bride *to the sinner*. Surely the sense requires us to regard this cry of "come" as addressed to our Lord Jesus, who in a previous verse had been saying, "Behold I come quickly, and my reward is with me." We may see the second included in it, but it will never do to exclude the first. We shall not have dealt honestly with the words before us unless we regard them first as spoken upward toward our Lord, whose coming is our great hope.

*The matter of this cry* is first to be noticed—it is the coming of Christ. "The Spirit and the bride say, Come." This is and always has been the universal cry of the church of Jesus Christ. There is no one common theory about the exact meaning of that coming, but there is one common desire for it, in some form or other. Some of us are expecting the bodily coming, because the angel said when the cloud concealed the rising Christ, "This same Jesus who is taken up from you into heaven shall so come in like manner as ye have seen him go into heaven." We therefore look for His descent upon the earth in person, to be here literally among us. Some expect that when He comes it will be to reign upon the earth, making all things new and bringing to His people a glorious period of a thousand years, in which there shall be perpetual Sabbath rest. Others think that when He cometh He will come to judge the world, and that the day of His appearing is rather to be regarded as the end of all things and the conclusion of this dispensation than as the commencement of the age of gold. There are some who think the millennium all a dream, and the coming of Christ in person to be a mere fancy, but they believe that He will come spiritually, and they are looking for a time when the gospel shall spread very wonderfully, and there will be an extraordinary power about the ministrations of the Word, so that nations shall run unto Him and be converted to His truth. Now it would be very interesting to take up these various statements and speculations, but we do not want to do so, because after all, in whatever way men look at it, all the true people of God still desire the coming of Christ, and so long as He draws near they are content. They may have more or less light about the manner of it, but still the coming of Christ has been ever since the time when He departed the great wish and desire, yea and the agonizing prayer of the church of God. "Even so, come quickly, Lord Jesus," is the cry of the whole host of the Lord's elect. It is true that some have not always desired this coming from motives of the most commendable kind, and many become more than ever earnest in this prayer when they have been in a state of disappointment and sorrow, but still that which they desire is a right thing, and a promised blessing to be given in its time. I suppose the file of sorrow will always give a keener edge to the desire of Christ's coming. Luther on one occasion, when much discouraged, said, "May the Lord come at once! Let Him cut the whole matter short with the day of judgment; for there is no amendment to be expected." When we get into this state of mind the desire, though right in appearance, may not be quite as pure as we think. Desires and prayers which grow out of unbelief and petulance can hardly be of the very best order. Perhaps when we more patiently wait and quietly hope, we may not be quite so feverishly anxious for the speedy coming, and yet our state of mind may be more sober and more truly watchful and acceptable than when we showed more apparent eagerness. Waiting must sit side by side with desiring: patience must blend with hope. The Lord's "quickly" may not be my "quickly"; and if so, let Him do what seemeth Him good. It may be a better thing after all for our Lord to tarry a little longer, that so by a more lengthened conflict He may the better manifest the patience of the saints and the power of the eternal Spirit. It may be the Lord may linger yet a while, and if so, while the church desires His speedy advent, she will not quarrel with her Master, nor dictate to Him, nor even wish to know the times and the seasons. "Come, Lord Jesus, come quickly," is her heart's inmost wish, but as for the details of His coming she leaves them in His hands.

Having noted the matter of the cry, let us next observe

*the persons crying.* The Spirit is first mentioned—"The Spirit and the bride say, Come." And why does the Holy Spirit desire the coming of the Lord Jesus? At present the Spirit is, so to speak, the vice-regent of this dispensation upon earth. Our Lord Jesus is gone into the heavens, for it was expedient for Him to go, but the Comforter whom the Father hath sent in His name hath taken His place as our teacher, and abides on earth continually as the witness to the truth, and the worker for it in the minds of men. But the Spirit of God is daily grieved during this season of long-suffering and conflict. How much He is provoked all the world over, it is not possible for us to know! The forty years in the wilderness must have become as nothing compared with nineteen centuries of rebellious generations. The ungodly vex Him, they reject His testimony, and resist His operations. And, alas, the saints grieve Him too. You and I have, I fear, grieved Him often during the past year; and so He desireth the end of this evil estate, and saith to our Lord Jesus, "Come." Besides, the Spirit's great object and desire is to glorify Christ, even as our Lord saith, "He shall glorify me, for he shall take of mine and shew them unto you." Now, as the coming of Christ will be the full manifestation of the Redeemer's glory, the Spirit therefore desireth that He may come and take to Himself His great power, and reign. The Holy Spirit seals us "unto the day of redemption," having ever an eye to that great event; His work tendeth toward its completion in the day of the appearing of the sons of God. He "is the earnest of our inheritance till the redemption of the purchased possession." Therefore doth the Spirit have sympathy in the groanings of His saints for the glorious appearing, and it is in this connection especially that He is described as helping our infirmities, and making intercession for us with groanings which cannot be uttered. In this sense the Spirit saith "Come"; indeed, all such cries of "Come" in this world are of His prompting.

Our text next tells us that, "the bride saith, Come." We all know that the bride is the church, but perhaps we have not noticed the peculiarity of her name. It is not "The Spirit and *the church* say, Come," but "the Spirit and the bride," for she saith "Come" always more fervently when she realizes her near and dear relationship to her Lord, and all that it involves. Now, a bride is one whose marriage is near, either as having just happened or as close at hand. She is far more than merely espoused—either she is married or about to be, although the actual marriage feast may not have been eaten. So is the church very nearly arrived at the grand hour, when it shall be said "the marriage of the Lamb is come and his bride hath made herself ready"; and because of that she is full of joy at the prospect of hearing the cry, "Behold, the Bridegroom cometh." Who marvelleth that it is so? It would be unnatural if there were no desire on the part of the church to see her beloved Lord and Head. Is it not as it should be when the bride saith "Come"?

I wish to call your attention to the fact that while I have made two of the persons mentioned in the text for the purpose of discoursing upon them in due order, yet they are not divided in the passage before us. It does not say the Spirit saith "come" and the bride saith "come," but "the Spirit and the bride say, Come." That is to say, the Spirit of God speaketh by the church when He crieth, "Come," and the church crieth unto Christ for His coming because she is moved thereto of the Holy Spirit. True prayer is always a joint work; the Holy Spirit within us writes acceptable desires upon our hearts and then we present them. The Holy Spirit does not plead apart from our desiring and believing: we must ourselves desire and will and plead and agonize because the Spirit of God worketh in us so to will and to do. We plead with God because we are prompted and guided by His Holy Spirit. Our pleadings, which go up to heaven for the advent of Jesus, are the Holy Spirit crying in the hearts of the blood-bought. The church herself prays in the Holy Spirit, instantly crying day and night for the fulfillment of the greatest of all the covenant promises.

The next clause of the text indicates that each separate believer should breathe the same desire, "Let him that heareth say, Come." Brethren, this will be the index of your belonging to the bride, the token of your sharing in the one Spirit, and being joined unto the one body, if you unite with the Spirit and the bride in saying, "Come." For no ungodly man truly desireth Christ's coming; but on the contrary he desireth to get away from Him, and forget His very existence. To delight in drawing near unto the Lord Jesus Christ is an evidence of our election and calling; to wish more and more fully to know Him and to dwell more near to Him is the token of our having been reconciled unto God by His death, and of our having a new nature implanted in us: to long to see Him manifested in fullness of glory is the ensign of a true soldier of the cross. Do you feel this? Do you desire to be better acquainted with the Lord Jesus? You have heard the gospel, do you say as the church doth, "Come, Lord Jesus"? Alas, to many the day of the Lord will be darkness and not light, and they cannot desire it, for it will be a day of terror and confusion unto them; but unto such as have heard and believed in the precious name of the Son of God it will be joy and peace, and therefore, the cry of their heart is, "Even so, come, Lord Jesus."

This utterance of "Come" by him that heareth it is the mark of his joyful consent to the fact that Christ shall come. It is well, my friend, if when thou hearest that Christ will come thou sayest, "Let him come." If He come to reign, let Him, for blessed be His name, who should reign but He? If He descend to judge the earth, let Him come, for we shall be justified at His bar. His ends and objects in coming cannot but be fraught with infinite benefit to us and glory to our God, and therefore, we would not delay His chariot wheels by so much as an hour.

The saying of "come" by each true hearer is the sign that his heart responds to the doctrine which he has been taught. We have received it by revelation that Christ is to come, and our soul saith, "Even so. Come Lord Jesus; it is our happiness that it should be so."

Thus have we mentioned the persons by whom this cry is uttered, and now let us add a word upon *the tense in which the cry is put*. It is in the present tense. "The Spirit and the bride say, Come. And let Him that heareth say, Come." The Spirit and the bride are anxious that Christ should come at once, and he that knoweth Christ and loveth Him desireth also that He should not tarry. Look, my brethren, is it not time as far as our poor judgments go that Jesus should come? See how iniquity abounds! Behold our very streets, how foul they are with sin! See how errors are multiplied: do they not swarm even in the church of God itself? Have not heresies come down like birds of prey upon the sacrifice, to pollute even the altars of the Most High? See at this present time how skeptics defy the living God, how they hiss out from between their teeth the question, "Where is the promise of his coming, for since the fathers fell asleep all things continue as they were?" Behold how Antichrist also stalks boldly through the land. Superstitions which your fathers could not bear are set up among you yet again, and the grave images, crosses, crucifixes and sacraments, gods many and lords many, of old Rome have come back to England again, and they are worshiped in her national church. In England, stained with the blood of martyrs, once again the mark of the beast is to be seen on the foreheads of those whom she feeds to teach systems of superstition, what else can shake ye from your thrones! O gods that have long ruled over superstitious minds, who else can hurl you to the moles and to the bats? Ye know Him who made you quiver on your thrones on that night when He was born in Bethlehem's manger, and ye may well tremble, for when He cometh it will be with an iron rod to dash you into shivers. "Even so," we cry, "come, Lord Jesus: come quickly. Amen."

## The Earthward Cry of Invitation to Men

II. Now, secondly, let us listen to the earthward cry of invitation to men. I must confess I cannot quite tell you how it is that the sense in my text glides away from the coming of Christ to the earth into the coming of sinners to Christ, but it does. Like colors which blend, or strains of music which melt into each other, so the first sense slides into the second. This almost insensible transition seems to me to have been occasioned by the memory of the fact that the coming of Christ is not desirable to all mankind.

There are the unbelievers who have not obeyed Him, and when they hear the Spirit and the bride say come, straightway they begin to tremble, and they say within themselves, "What if he should come! Alas, we rejected him, and his coming will be our destruction." I think I hear some such sinners weeping and wailing at the very thought of the Lord's coming, for they know that they also who have pierced Him must behold Him and weep because of Him. It seems almost cruel on the part of the bride and the Spirit to be saying come, when that coming must be for the overthrow of all the adversaries of the Lord: and so Jesus Himself seems gently to turn aside the prayer of His people while He pleads with the needy ones. He lets the prayer flow toward Himself, but yet directs its flow toward poor sinners also. He Himself seems to say, "Ye bid me come, but I, as the Savior of men, look at your brothers and your sisters who are yet in the far country, the other sheep which are not yet of the fold, whom also I must bring in, and in answer to your cry to me to come I speak to those wandering ones, and say, 'Let him that is athirst come, and whosoever will, let him take the water of life freely.'" Is not that the way in which the sense glides from its first direction?

Now, *from whom does this cry arise*?

It first comes *from Jesus*. It is He who says, "Let him that is athirst come." The passage so stands, as I have already said, that we cannot but believe this verse to have been the utterance of Him who is the root and offspring of David, and the bright and morning star. He out of heaven cries to the unconverted, "Let him that is athirst come." Will they refuse Him that speaketh? Shall Jesus Himself invite them and will they turn a deaf ear?

But next, it is the call of *the Spirit of God*. The Spirit says, "Come." This Book which He has written, on every page says to men, "Come! Come to Jesus." This is the cry of the Spirit in the preaching of the Word. What mean sermons and discourses but "Come sinner, come?" And those secret motions of power upon the conscience, those times when the heart grows calm even amid dissipation, and thought is forced upon the mind, those are the movements of the Spirit of God by which He is showing man His danger and revealing to him His refuge, and so is saying, "Come." All over the world wherever there is a Bible and a preacher the Spirit is saying "Come."

And this is the speech of *the church* too in conjunction with the Spirit, for the Spirit speaks with the bride and the bride speaks by the Spirit. The church is always saying "Come." This is indeed the meaning of her Sabbath gatherings, of her testimony in the pulpit, of her teaching in the schools, of her prayers and her exhortations. Everywhere, poor wandering hearts, the church of God is saying to you, "Come"; or if she does not do so she is not acting in her true character as the bride of Christ. For this purpose is there a church in the world at all; if it were not for this our Lord might take His people home as soon as they have believed, but they are kept here to be a seed to keep the truth alive in the world, and their daily earnest cry to you is "Come, come to Jesus." "The Spirit and the bride say, Come."

The next giver of the invitation is spoken of as "*him that heareth*." If you have had an ear to hear, and have heard the gospel to your own salvation, the very next thing you have to do is to say to those around you, "Come." Go and speak to anybody that you meet, to everybody that you meet, according as opportunity and occasion shall be given you, and say what all the church saith and what the Spirit is saying—namely, "Come." Give your Master's invitation, distribute the testimony of His loving will, and bid poor sinners come to Jesus. Your children and your servants—bid them come; your neighbors and your friends—bid them come; the strangers and the far-off ones—bid them come; the harlot and the thief—bid such come; those that are in the highways and the hedges, those who are far-off from God by abominable works—say also unto all these "Come." Because you have heard the message and proved its truth, go you and call in others to the feast of love. Oh, if there were more of these individual proclaimers what blessings would descend upon London! I do not know how many believers in Christ there are present in this house, but I do know that there are five thousand of us associated in church fellowship at this Tabernacle; and if the whole of these five thousand would but begin to bear witness for Christ with all their might, there would be salt enough even within this one house to season all London, with God's blessing upon our efforts. My brothers and sisters, let us not be slow to address ourselves to those to whom the Spirit of God within us, and the voice of Jesus from above, and the cry of the whole church is addressed. Let each individual member take up the note of invitation till all around the trembling sinner hears the encouraging cry of "Come."

Now, notice the *remarkably encouraging character of this "Come,"* which is given by the Spirit and the bride. One part of it is directed to the thirsty: "Let him that is athirst come." By thirst is meant necessity, and an appetite for its supply. Dost thou feel thyself guilty, and dost thou desire pardon?—thou art a thirsty one. Art thou disquieted and filled with unrest, and dost thou long to be pacified in heart?—thou art a thirsty one. Is there a something, thou knowest not perhaps what it is, for which thou art sighing, and crying, and pining?—thou art a thirsty one, and to thee is the invitation most positively and distinctly given, "Let him that is athirst come."

But how much I rejoice that the second half of the invitation does not contain even an apparent limit, as this first sentence has been thought to do! I regard the thirst here mentioned as by no means requiring of any man that he should have gone through a process of horror on account of guilt, or should have been overwhelmed with conviction, and driven to despair of salvation. I believe that any desire and any longing will come under the description of "thirst"; but since some have stumbled at it, and have said again and again, "I feel I do not thirst enough," see how sweetly the second clause of our text puts it—"Whosoever will, let him take the water of life freely." Whether thou be thirsty or not, yet hast thou a will to drink? hast thou a will to be saved? a will to be cleansed from sin? a will to be made a new creature in Christ Jesus? Dost thou will to have eternal life? Then thus saith the Spirit to thee, "Whosoever will, let him take the water of life freely."

Now, notice three vast doors through which the hugest and most elephantine sinner that ever made the earth shake beneath the weight of his guilt may go. Here are the three doors. *"Whosoever"—"will"—"freely."* "Whosoever," there is the first door. "Whosoever"—then what man dare have the impudence to say that he is shut out? If you say that you cannot come in under *"whosoever,"* I ask you how you dare narrow a word which is in itself so broad, so infinite. "Whosoever"—that must mean every man that ever lived, or ever shall live, while yet he is here and wills to come. Well, then, the word *"will."* There is nothing about past character, nor present character; nothing about knowledge, or feeling, nor anything else but the will: "Whosoever will." Speak of the gate standing ajar! This looks to me like taking the door right off the hinges and carrying it away. "Whosoever will." There is no hindrance whatever in your way. And then *"freely."* God's gifts are given without any expectation or recompense, or any requirements and conditions—"Let him take the water of life freely." Thou hast not to bring thy good feelings, or good desires, or good works, but come and take freely what God gives you for nothing. You are not even to bring repentance and faith in order to obtain grace, but you are to come and accept repentance and faith as the gifts of God, and the work of the Holy Spirit. What broad gates of mercy these are! How wide the entrance which love has prepared for coming souls! *"Whosoever!" "Will!" "Freely!"*

Observe how the invitation sums up the work the sinner is called upon to do. First, he is bidden to *come*. "Whosoever will, let him come." Now, to come to Christ means simply for the soul to draw near to Him by trusting Him. You are not asked to bring a load with you, nor to work for Christ in order to salvation, but just to come to Him. Nothing is said about the style of coming, come running or creeping, come boldly or timidly, for if you do but come to Jesus, He will in no wise cast you out. A simple reliance upon the Lord Jesus is the one essential for eternal life.

Then the next direction is *"take."* "Whosoever will, let him take." That is all. That word "take" is a grand word to express the gospel. The world's gospel is "bring": Christ's gospel is "take." Nature's grace which is "take." There is the water, dear friends, you have not to dig a well to find it, you have only to take it. There is the bread of heaven, you have not to grind the flour or bake the loaf, you have only to take it. There is a garment woven from the top throughout, and without seam; you have not to add a fringe to it, you have only to take it. The way of salvation may be summed up in the four letters of the word "take." Do you desire Christ? take Him. Do you want pardon? take it. Do you need a new heart? take it. Do you want peace on earth? take it. Do you want heaven hereafter? take it—that is all. "Whosoever will, let him *take* the water of life freely."

And there is one other word which I love to dwell on, and it comes twice over: "*let him* that is athirst come, and whosoever will *let him* take." It is graciously said, *let him*. It seems to me as if the Lord Jesus Christ saw a poor soul standing thirsty at the flowing crystal fountain of His love, and the devil standing there whispered to him, "You see the sacred stream, but it flows for others. It is what you need, but you must not have it, it is not for you." Listen, there is a voice from beyond the clouds which cries aloud, "Let him take it!" Stand back, devil, let the willing one come! He is putting down his lip to drink—he understands it now—but there comes rushing upon him a host of his old sins like so many winged harpies, and they scream out to him, "Go back, you must not draw nigh, this fountain is not for you: this pure crystal stream must not be defiled by such leprous lips as yours." Again there comes from the throne of love this blessed password, "Let him come and let him take." It is as when a man is in court and is called for, to go into the witness-box. He is standing in the crowd, and his name is called: what happens? As soon as he hears his name he begins to push through the throng to reach his place. "What are you at?" says one. "I am called," says he. "Stand back; why do you push so?" says another. "I am called by the judge," says he. A big policeman demands, "Why are you making such confusion in court?" "But," says the man, "I am called. My name was called out, and I must come." If he cannot come, if it is not possible for him to get through the throng, one of the authorities calls out, "Make way for that man—he is summoned by the court. Officers, clear a passage and let him come." Now the Lord Jesus calls the thirsty one and He says, "Whosoever will, let him come!" Make way doubts, make way sins, make way fears, make way devils, make way all of you for Jesus Christ the great king and judge of all has said, "Let him come!" Who shall hinder when Jesus permits? He who is divinely called shall surely come to Jesus. Come he shall, whoever may stand in his way. This morning I feel as if I could come to Jesus over again, and I will do so. Do you not feel the same, my beloved brethren? Well then, dear brother or sister, after you have so done turn round and proclaim this precious gospel invitation to all around you, and say to them "Come and take the water of life freely."

## The Connection Between These Two Comings

III. The third point is the connection between these two comings. Is there any relation between the coming of Christ from heaven to earth, and the coming of poor sinful creatures to Christ and trusting Him?

There is this relation, first, they are both suggested in this passage, by the closing of the scriptural canon. John is about to write by the voice of the Lord that none are to add to or take from the completed Book of God. The church says, "If there are no more prophets to proclaim the mind of God, no more apostles to write with infallible authority, and no more instructors to give forth new revelations, or bring new promises, then it only remaineth that the Lord should come. "Then," says she, "Come, Lord Jesus." And here are the sinners standing round, and they hear that no other gospel is to be expected, no more revelations are to be added to those which are in this book, there will be no other atonement, no other way of salvation, therefore it is their wisdom to come at once to Jesus. It is because the Book was about to receive its *finis* that the Spirit and the bride unitedly cried to the sinners to come at once. No fresh gospel is to be expected, therefore let them come at once. Why should they tarry any longer? The oxen and fatlings are killed, come to the supper! All things are ready, there is nothing more to be done, or to be revealed; upon us the ends of the earth have come. "It is finished" hath rung through earth and heaven, therefore:

> "Come and welcome, sinner come!"

I think I perceive another connection, namely, that those people who in very truth love Christ enough to cry to Him continually to come are sure to love sinners also, and to say to them also, "Come." Not but what there are some who talk a great deal about Christ's coming, and yet manifest but small care for other men's souls. Well, it is talk; the profession of looking for the second advent is nothing but talk when it does not lead people to cry to perishing men, "Come to Christ." He who loves Christ so very much that he is quite wrapped up in himself, and forgets the dying millions around him, and stands star-gazing into heaven, expecting to see a sudden glory, to take himself away, does not understand what he saith: for if he loved his Lord he would set to work for Him, and would show that he expected the King to come by endeavoring to extend His kingdom.

There is this connection also, that before Christ comes a certain number of His elect must be ingathered. He shall not come until an appointed company shall have been brought to eternal life by the preaching of the Word. Oh then, brethren, it is ours to labor that the wanderers may come home, for so we are, as far as lieth in us, hastening the time when our Beloved Himself shall come.

Once more, there is a sort of coming of Christ which, though it be not the first meaning here, may be included in it, for it touches the center of the sinner's coming to Christ. Because, brethren, when we cry, "Come, Lord Jesus," if He shall answer us by giving us of His Spirit more fully, so that He comes to us spiritually, then penitent souls will assuredly be brought to His feet. We know this, that wherever the Lord Himself is in a meeting, hearts are sure to be broken and repentance is certain to be manifested. Wherever Jesus Christ is in power there must be a revival, for dead souls must come to life in

Him. The great thing we want above all others is a grip to that glorious promise, "Lo, I am with you alway, even to the end of the world," and as we in this sense obtain the coming of the Lord, we shall see sinners come and take of the water of life.

### What Are the Responses?

IV. Well then, lastly, what are the responses? We sent up a cry to heaven, and said, "Come." The response is, "Behold, I come quickly." That is eminently satisfactory. You may have to wait awhile, but the cry is heard, and if the Lord should not come in your lifetime, the same preparation of heart which made you look for His coming will be blessedly useful to you if He sends His messenger to take you home by death. The same waiting and watching will answer in either case, so you need not be under any distress about which of the two shall happen. Christ will descend to earth as surely as He ascended to heaven, and when He cometh there will be victory to the right and to the true, and His saints shall reign with Him.

And now concerning this other cry of "Come." We ask sinners to come. We have asked them in a fourfold voice: Jesus, the Spirit, the bride, and him that heareth, they have all said, "Come." Will they come? Brethren and sisters, it is a question which I cannot answer. You must not ask *me*, for I do not know; but you had better ask the persons themselves: they are of age, ask *them*. Take care that you do ask them, my dear friends, I do trust that this last day of the year may be to you a day of mercy. The Jews had a feast of ingatherings at the end of the year, and I earnestly pray that we may have an ingathering of precious souls to Christ ere the year quite runs out: that would be a grand finish to this year of grace, and a sweet encouragement for the future.

But suppose you do not come. Well, you have been invited. If a Christmas feast is provided for the poor, and a number of beggars are standing shivering outside in the sleet and snow, and will not come in though earnestly bidden, we say, "Well, you have been invited: what more do you want?" Remember, also, that you have been invited very earnestly. The Spirit, the bride, and him that heareth, and Jesus Himself, they have all said to you, "Come." I am as the man that heareth, and I have said, "Come." I do not know how to say it more earnestly than I have said it. Oh, how would my soul delight if every one here did come to Christ at this moment! I would ask no greater joy out of heaven to crown this year with. You are invited, and you are earnestly invited, what more do you want! If you never come, you will have this thought to haunt you forever—"I was invited and pressed again and again, but I would not come."

I want you to remember, too, that you are called to come now, at once. You may not be bidden to come tomorrow for several reasons: you may not be alive, or there may be no earnest person near you to invite you. Can there be a better day today? You have always said "Tomorrow," yet where are you now? Not a bit forwarder some of you than you were ten years ago. Do you recollect that sermon when you were made to tremble so, and you said, "Please God, if I get out of this, I will seek his face," but you postponed it, and are you any forwarder now? You remember the story of the countryman who would not cross the river just yet, but sat down and said he would wait until all the water had gone by. He waited long in vain, and he might have waited forever, for rivers are always flowing. You too are waiting till a more convenient season shall come, and all the difficulties shall have gone by. Be quit of such supreme folly. There always will be difficulty, the river will always flow. O man, be wise, plunge into it and swim across. Now is the accepted time, and now is the day of salvation. Oh that you would believe in Jesus Christ! May His Spirit lead you to do so now.

> "Only trust him! only trust him!
> Only trust him *now*!
> He will save you! he will save you!
> He will save you *now*!"

Cast yourselves upon the blood and merits of the Lord Jesus, and the great work is done. The Lord help you to do so. Amen.

## Behold, a White Horse

**Clarence Edward Noble Macartney** (1879-1957) ministered in Paterson, New Jersey, and Philadelphia, Pennsylvania, before assuming the influential pastorate of First Presbyterian Church, Pittsburgh, where he ministered for twenty-seven years. His preaching especially attracted men, not only to the Sunday services but also to his popular Tuesday noon luncheons. He was gifted in dealing with Bible biographies, and, in this respect, has well been called "the American Alexander Whyte." Much of his preaching was topical-textual, but it was always biblical, doctrinal and practical. Perhaps his most famous sermon is "Come Before Winter."

The sermon I have selected is taken from *The Greatest Texts of the Bible*, published 1947 by Abingdon-Cokesbury Press, republished by Kregel Publications, 1992.

## Clarence Edward Noble Macartney

# 4

# BEHOLD, A WHITE HORSE

> And I saw heaven opened, and behold, a white horse; and he that sat upon him was called Faithful and True (Revelation 19:11).

MILAN, ITALY, A FAMOUS CITY on the Lombard Plain, is a place of stirring memories. In the ruins of the church of St. Ambrogio you recall how Ambrose there refused Theodosius the sacrament because of his massacre of the populace at Thessalonica. When the emperor protested, by way of extenuation, that David was both a murderer, and an adulterer, Ambrose said to him, "You have imitated David in his crime; now imitate him in his repentance." Your heart thrills to remember that under that same blue sky, and perhaps on the very spot over which you are walking, the Holy Spirit was His mighty conquest over the soul of Augustine. In the refectory of the monastery of Santa Maria della Grazie you can see the poor ghost of Leonardo da Vinci's "Last Supper." But the chief glory of Milan is its cathedral, and in some respects its most beautiful, stretching out before you. The 52 marble columns which hold up the lofty octagonal dome, and the 4,440 turrets, pinnacles, and the statues of angels and saints produce an incomparable combination of grace and grandeur, beauty and vastness.

Passing behind the high altar, you are suddenly confronted by one of the largest stained-glass windows in the world, like a window opened in heaven. The afternoon sun streaming through the window turns it into a sea of glass mingled with fire, whereon are depicted, not the scenes of the Old Testament, the Creation, the Fall, the Flood, Abraham, Jacob, Joseph, Moses, Elijah, David, the judges, the kings, and the prophets; nor the scenes of the Gospels, the Incarnation, the Temptation, the Denial, the

Transfiguration, the Betrayal, the Crucifixion, the Resurrection, and the Ascension; nor scenes from the Acts, the preaching of the apostles and the spread of the gospel; but the tremendous imagery of the Apocalypse—the sounding trumpets, the outpoured vials, Michael and his angels in battle with the dragon and his angels, the star Wormwood falling out of heaven, the great angel with the rainbow upon his head, standing with one foot on the sea and the other on the earth, and swearing by Him that liveth forever and ever that time shall be no longer, the woman clothed with the sun and the moon under her feet, Satan bound with a chain and cast into the bottomless pit, the great white throne, and, most impressive of all, the white horse and his rider going forth conquering and to conquer, with the armies of heaven in his train.

There are things in the book of Revelation which we cannot understand and about which we cannot be sure, but there are many things that we can understand. When you behold the fall of Babylon, lamented on earth and celebrated in heaven, when you see the overthrow of the false prophet and the beast and the dragon, when you behold the white horse and his rider, His vesture dipped in blood, with many crowns upon His head, and on His vesture and on His thigh a name written—King of Kings and Lord of Lords—you know that what you are beholding is the victory of the Kingdom of Christ.

Come then with me into this glorious cathedral of our faith, and with the lights and tumults of the world shut out let us contemplate the triumph of Christ. Let us behold first the certainty of the triumph of Christ and the necessity of an invincible faith in that triumph, and second how that triumph will come through Christ, by Christ, and for Christ alone.

### The Certainty of the Triumph

When the seamen that night on Paul's shipwrecked vessel knew that they were driving toward some shore, they must have wondered just how that voyage was going to end. So we wonder about the end of the world drift, the end of world history. "Then cometh the end" was the great utterance of the Apostle Paul. The end is just as logical and inevitable as the beginning. All objects and processes of nature, as we behold them, have not only a beginning but an ending. The day dawns, the sun runs his course and sinks beyond the horizon, and the day is ended. The night begins. The moon and the stars come up. At length they fade and disappear. The shadows depart, the day begins to dawn. The night is ended. The tiny rivulet begins to flow high up on the mountain ridge and becomes the great river which blesses the earth with its waters. At length the river loses itself in the ocean. The river has come to an end. The Bible, and the Bible alone, tells us of a great and glorious end to human history. It is there that we see the great movement toward righteousness reaching its climax in the Kingdom of God. The splendor of that climax is reflected in the book of Revelation, and nowhere is that splendor more overcoming than in this vision of the white horse and his rider, with the armies of heaven in His train.

In his great sermon on "Suffering for Christ," John Calvin said: "All the exhortations which can be given us to suffer for the name of Jesus Christ and in defense of the gospel, will have no effect if we do not feel sure of the cause for which we fight." That assurance of the victory of our cause is granted to us in the Apocalypse. This vision of victory is necessary for our faith and endurance and hope. You and I in our day see too little and, at the same time, too much, and often what we do see seems stronger than what we believe. Hence we must have the supplement of the book of Revelation, where we see the triumph of the truth and principles which are elsewhere declared in the Scriptures. Thus it is that no preacher has sounded the highest note until he has echoed the trumpet of the Apocalypse. No preacher has stood upon the highest ground till he has stood here and looked down the long corridors of time until those corridors converge in the Kingdom of God. It is here that we see the rainbow which spans the stormy sky of human history, and it is here that we listen to the melodized thunder of the last great day when the kingdoms of this world shall have become the kingdoms of our Lord, and of His Christ—a day so splendid that, compared with it, the brightest day that has hitherto shone upon the world is but midnight, and the fairest splendors which have invested it are but the shadow of darkness.

If this vision of the triumph of Christ was necessary for the church and the Roman Empire when that pagan empire was striving to drown the church in its own blood, it is not less necessary for us today when Antichrist has invented new masks for his face and has multiplied his lies and his perversions of the truth.

> Our Lord is still rejected
> And by this world disowned;
> By the many still neglected
> And by the few enthroned.

There are times when the heart grows dull and heavy with the deadly monotony of evil in the world. The origin of evil troubles us. Why did God permit it? We try to answer that by saying that for a moral being there must be the freedom of choice and, therefore, the possibility of evil. The continuance of evil troubles us. In John's vision the beast, who had received his death stroke and had hid for a time spouting blood, emerged at length from the abyss with his death stroke healed, and the whole world wandered after the beast and worshiped him. So evil in the hearts of men and in human institutions is constantly re-emerging and re-incarnating itself, its death stroke healed. We comfort ourselves with the thought that God is able to bring good out of evil, but still we shall ask ourselves: Is God not omnipotent? Is God not all good? And if so, why did he permit evil in the beginning? Why does he not destroy it not? The great answer that the Bible gives us, and the answer of this vision, is the certainty of the destruction and overthrow of evil. When Robinson Crusoe's man Friday wanted to know why God did not destroy the Devil, the answer that Crusoe finally gave him was the right answer, and the only answer, and the great answer: "God will destroy him." We see the ebb and flow of progress and decay, the unfolding of the long and bloody panorama of history, humanity's aspiration of the best and its doing of the worst. We see the church in ceaseless battle with the beast. But that is not all we see. Look at this window! Here you see the end of evil—"Then cometh the end." You see the Lamb of God standing upon Mount Zion. You see all things put under His feet. You see the white horse and his rider, with the armies of heaven in His train and many crowns upon His head. You see this world of strife and toil and envy and hate and sin and passion and blood and death give way to the new heavens and the new earth, wherein dwelleth righteousness, not as a fugitive visitor, but as the eternal and unbroken order.

## The Triumph of Christ

The triumph of righteousness will come for Christ, by Christ, and through Christ alone. Men look forward to a golden age, to the triumph of justice and righteousness and the benediction of universal peace. But how will this come about? "Then cometh the end." But by what means will the end come?

It will not come through any natural growth or development. There are those who speak as if they think that is the way by which we shall reach the millennial age. They believe there is a law of irresistible and invincible progress at work in the world and running through the ages. The ape and the tiger will die in man. The tide of justice and good will and righteousness will rise higher and higher until the whole earth shall be covered with its flood. They tell us to look back over the past by which man has come. Behold the broken fetters which he cast aside. Behold the bones and skeletons of the systems of iniquity and wickedness which man has overthrown and destroyed. All that man needs is time, and progress counts time in ages. Progress takes one step and the age have elapsed. With progress one day is as a thousand years, and a thousand years as one day.

But this theory, this hypothesis of unstoppable and invincible progress, regardless of what men and nations do, regardless of the moral law, crumbles before fact. This theory received a rude shock in World War I, and World War II almost destroyed it.

If there is progress, there is also retrogression. If there is construction, there is also destruction. The great French entomologist Fabre, after tracing the advance of human knowledge, asks:

"To what an ideal height will this process and evolution lead mankind? To no very magnificent height, it is to be feared. We are afflicted with an indelible taint, a sort of original sin. We are made after a pattern and can do nothing to change ourselves. We are marked with the mark of the beast, the taint of the belly, the inexhaustible source of bestiality."

If all we have to count on for the future is natural progress, education, and science, then all we can expect is the perpetual recurrence of what is and what has been, the truceless battle between light and darkness, the eternal conflict over the body of mankind, as Michael and the Devil disputed over the body of Moses. Is there any evidence that science, even should it conquer those three great scourges of man's body, heart disease, tuberculosis, and cancer, will ever stop men from dying? Will progress ever stop men from sinning? Can knowledge ever wipe away all tears from our eyes or heal the broken heart? To ask these questions is to answer them.

Others hold that the great end—the triumph of righteousness and peace—will come, not through any natural law of progress and evolution, but through the expansion and development of the spiritual forces which are now at work in this world through the church. The world, they remind us, is bad enough with Christianity. What would it be without it? Think of the changes which have been enacted. Think of the progress that has been made. Think of the promises that are given. Did Christ not say that the kingdom of heaven "is like unto leaven, which a woman took, and hid in three measures of meal, till the whole was leavened"? Did He not say that the kingdom of heaven "is like to a grain of mustard seed, which a man took, and sowed in his field: which is indeed the least of all seeds: but when it is grown, it is the greatest among herbs, and becometh a tree, so that the birds of the air come and lodge in the branches thereof"? Was not the vision given unto Ezekiel of the healing waters which issued from under the threshold of the holy house—first up to the ankles, then up to the knees, then up to the loins, then a river to swim in, a river that could not be passed, a river which brought life wherever it flowed and healed the waters of the Dead Sea? Do we not have there the picture of the gradual conquest of the world through the expansion of the spiritual forces now in the church? Do these not point to the day when "righteousness shall be the girdle of his loins and faithfulness the girdle of his reins. The wolf also shall dwell with the lamb, and the leopard shall lie down with the kid; . . . and the sucking child shall play on the hole of the asp, and the weaned child shall put his hand on the cockatrice's den. They shall not hurt nor destroy in all my holy mountain: for the earth shall be full of the knowledge of the Lord, as the waters cover the sea"?

These are indeed great and beautiful promises, and a great encouragement to the church in its work. But there is more to reckon with than a gradual growth and spread of righteousness. Whatever those figures used by Christ mean, the opened heaven, the shaken earth, travail, anguish and woe, the sun turned into darkness and the moon into blood, certainly they do not indicate a slow, gradual ripening into perfection. In that same address and among those other parables of the Kingdom, like the mustard seed and the leaven in the measures of meal, there is the brief but profound parable of the wheat and the tares. When the servants of the householder asked permission to pull up the tares, He said, "Let them both grow together until the harvest." This tells us that there is a growth and development of evil as well as good. The wheat and the tares grow side by side unto the harvest. Neither wheat nor tares can harvest themselves. Our Lord, after He encouraged men to pray by the parable of the unjust judge, and gave assurance that God will avenge His own elect, asked, that solemn question, with the implied negative answer, "When the Son of man cometh, shall he find faith on the earth?"

No, the final victory will come, not through natural progress, not through the expansion of the religious forces now at work in the world, but through another mighty act of God. Whatever the intermediate steps may be, whatever the ebb and flow of progress, the end will come, not by the improvement or the development of the present order, but through the complete supercession of it. The climax of history will be the appearance on the field of battle of the captain of our salvation himself, and the glory of it will be comparable to what John beheld—the white horse and his rider going forth conquering and to conquer, with many crowns upon His head.

When the army of Julian the Apostate was on the march to Persia, some of the soldiers were tormenting and torturing a Christian believer. Wearying at length of their brutal sport, they looked down on their helpless victim and asked him with infinite scorn, "Where now is your Carpenter-God?" The man looked up at them through his blood and tears and answered, "He is making a coffin for your emperor." Yes, for every God-defying person and power and principle, for all that exalts itself against God and His Word, the coffin is now preparing. When Christ comes as conqueror, He shall pronounce the divine doom upon all wicked civilization and all inhuman forms of cruelty and lust, and upon all the enemies of God and righteousness, not only partially and locally, as hitherto, just enough to show us that there is a God who judges, but universally, in the whole created world. Once He was despised and rejected of men; then every knee shall bow. Once men railed on Him with their tongue; then every tongue shall confess that Christ is Lord. Once He was dumb with silence; then His voice shall shake both the heavens and the earth. Once they put a crimson robe on Him and mocked Him; then He will wear the crimson vesture of His triumphant atonement. Once twelve humble men followed Him about; then the armies of heaven will follow in His train. Once they pressed a crown of thorns upon His brow; then He will wear many crowns upon His head.

Some time again the train on which I was traveling stopped at Ashtabula, Ohio. At once my mind recalled the great railroad disaster of 1876, when a train went through the bridge there taking the lives of many people, among them the famous evangelist and singer and composer of hymns, P. P. Bliss. One of his best-known hymns is "Hold the Fort." After the fall of Atlanta, in July, 1864, General John B. Hood, the commander of the Confederate army, marched westward to attack the communications of Sherman with Chattanooga and Nashville, hoping to draw back Sherman's army from Georgia. One of the posts he attacked was Allatoona Pass, commanded by the brave and capable General Corse. Sherman himself went back with part of his army as far as Kenesaw Mountain, where a battle had been fought some months before. From the summit of the mountain he heliographed to the beleaguered garrison at Allatoona Pass, "Hold the fort! I am coming!" In Sherman's army at the time was a Major Whittle, afterward a well-known evangelist. Whittle related the incident to Bliss, who, taking it for his inspiration, wrote the hymn:

> "Hold the fort, for I am coming,"
> Jesus signals still;
> Wave the answer back to heaven,
> "By thy grace we will."

The message of Christ to His church is "Occupy till I come!" He may come at the midnight watch. He may come in the third watch. He may come in the fourth watch, as He came that night walking over the waves to the disciples in the storm-driven ship on Galilee's Sea. But whatever hour He comes, "Blessed are those servants, whom the Lord when he cometh shall find watching: verily I say unto you, that he shall gird himself, and make them to sit down to meat, and will come forth and serve them." What a day that will be! Then none shall be sorry that he fought the good fight and finished the course and kept the faith.

Lift up your hearts! Our King shall come! Our cause shall conquer! When the world sky is darkest with clouds of unbelief, behold the glory of the coming of the Lord. Above all the chariots and horsemen of this world, behold the white horse and his rider; and when the babel sounds are loudest in their scornful derision of God and His eternal Son, you shall hear floating down from heaven the notes of that distant triumph song whose sweet melody shall one day encompass the heavens and the earth, "Alleluia: for the Lord God omnipotent reigneth!" "The kingdoms of this world are become the kingdoms of our Lord, and of his Christ; and he shall reign forever and ever."

# NOTES

## Christ's House and Servants—His Second Coming

**Robert Murray McCheyne** (1813-1843) is one of the brightest lights of the Church of Scotland. Born in Dundee, he was educated in Edinburgh and licensed to preach in 1835. For a brief time, he assisted his friend Andrew A. Bonar at Larbert and Dunipace. In 1836 he was ordained and installed as pastor of St. Peter's Church, Dundee, where he served until his untimely death two months short of his thirtieth birthday. He was known for his personal sanctity and his penetrating ministry of the Word, and great crowds came to hear him preach. *The Memoirs and Remains of Robert Murray McCheyne*, by Andrew Bonar, is a Christian classic that every minister of the gospel should read.

This sermon is taken from *The Additional Remains of the Rev. Robert Murray McCheyne*, published in 1846 in Edinburgh by William Oliphant and Company.

**Robert Murray McCheyne**

# 5

# CHRIST'S HOUSE AND SERVANTS— HIS SECOND COMING

> For the Son of Man is as a man taking a far journey, who left his house, and gave authority to his servants, and to every man his work, and commanded the porter to watch. Watch ye therefore: for ye know not when the master of the house cometh, at even, or at midnight, or at cockcrowing, or in the morning: lest coming suddenly he find you sleeping. And what I say unto you, I say unto all, Watch (Mark 13:34-37).

I. *The Church on earth is Christ's house*: "Who left his house" (v. 34). This parable represents the church on earth as Christ's home or dwelling.

A. *Because He is the foundation stone of it.* Just as every stone of a building rests on the foundation, so does every believer rest on Christ. He is the foundation rock upon which they rest. If it were not for the foundation, the whole house would fall into ruins—the floods and winds would sweep it away. If it were not for Christ, all believers would be swept away by God's anger; but they are rooted and built up in Him, and so they form His house.

B. *Because He is the builder.* (1.) Every stone of the building has been placed there by the hands of Christ—Christ has taken every stone from the quarry. Look unto the rock whence ye were hewn, and the hold of the pit whence ye were digged. A natural person is embedded in the world just as firmly as a rock in the quarry. The hands of the almighty Savior alone can dig out the soul, and loosen it from its natural state. (2.) Christ has carried it, and laid it on the foundation. Even when a stone has been quarried, it cannot lift itself; it needs to be carried, and built upon the foundation. So when a natural soul has been wakened, He cannot build himself on Christ; he must be carried on the shoulder of the great master builder. Every stone of the building!

Well may it be called Christ's house, when He builds every stone of it. See that ye be quarried out by Christ; see to it, that ye be carried by Him—built on Him; then you will be an habitation of God through the Spirit.

C. *Because His friends are in it.* Wherever a man's friends are, that is his home—wherever a man's mother and sister and brother dwell, that is his home; this, then, must be Christ's home, for He stretched forth His hand toward His disciples, and said: "Behold my mother and my brethren; for whosoever shall do the will of my Father which is in heaven, the same is my brother, and sister, and mother." As long as this world has a believer in it, Christ will look upon it as His house. He cannot forget, even in glory, the well of Samaria—the garden of Gethsemane—the hill of Calvary. Happy for you who know Christ, and who do the will of His Father; wherever you dwell, Christ calls it His house. You may dwell in a poor place, and still be happy; for Christ dwells with you, and calls it His dwelling—He calls you "My brother, sister, mother."

II. *Christ is like a man who has gone a far journey* (v. 34). Although the church on earth be His house, and although He has such affection for it, yet Christ is not here, He is risen—Christ is risen indeed.

A. *He has gone to take possession of heaven in our name.* When an elder brother of a family purchases a property for himself and his brothers, he goes a far journey, in order to take possession. So Christ is an elder brother. He lived and died in order to purchase forgiveness and acceptance for sinners. He has gone into heaven to take possession for us. Do you take Christ for your surety? Then you are already possessed of heaven.

*Ques.* How am I possessed of heaven, when I have never been there?

*Ans.* Christ your surety has taken possession in your name. If you realize this, it will give you fullness of joy. A person may possess a property which he has never seen.

Look at your surety in the land that is very far off, calling it all His own, for the sake of his younger brethren: "These things have I spoken unto you, that your joy may be full."

B. *He has gone to intercede for us.* (1.) He has gone to intercede for unawakened, barren sinners: "Lord, let it alone this year also." Oh, sinner! why is it that you have not died a sudden death? Why have you not gone quite down into the pit? How often the Savior has prayed for some of you! Shall it be all in vain? (2.) To intercede for His believing people—to procure all blessings for them. Often an elder brother of a family goes into a far country, and sends back rich presents to his younger brethren at home. This is what Christ has done. He has gone far above all heavens, there to appear in the presence of God for us, and to ask the very things we need, and to send us down all the treasures of heaven. Of His fullness have we all received, even grace for grace. "I will pray the Father, and he shall give you another Comforter." Oh, Christians! believe in a praying Christ, if you would receive heavenly blessings. Believe just as if you say Him, and open the mouth wide to receive the blessings for which He is praying.

C. *He has gone to prepare a place for us.* When a family is going to emigrate to a foreign shore, often the elder brother goes before to prepare a place for his younger brethren. This is what Christ has done. He does not intend that we should live here always—He has gone a far journey in order to prepare a place for us: "I go to prepare a place for you; and if I go and prepare a place for you, I will come again and receive you to myself, that where I am, there ye may be also." Oh, Christians! believe in Christ preparing a place for you. It will greatly take away the fear of dying. It is an awful thing to die, even for a forgiven and sanctified soul—to enter on a world unknown, unseen, untried. One thing takes away fear: Christ is preparing a place quite suitable for my soul—He knows all the wants and weaknesses of my frame—I know He will make it a pleasant home to me.

III. *All Christ's people are servants, and have their work assigned them* (v. 34).

A. *Ministers are servants, and have their work assigned them.* Two kinds are here mentioned. (1.) Stewards. These seem to be the servants to whom He gave authority. All ministers should be stewards—rightly dividing the Word of life—giving to everyone of the family his portion of meat in due season. Oh! it is a blessed work, to feed the church of God, which He hath purchased with His own blood—to give milk to babes, and strong meat to grown men—to give convenient food to everyone. Pray for your ministers, that they may be made faithful and wise stewards. There are few such. (2.) Porters. He commanded the porter to watch. It is the office of some ministers to stand at the door and invite every sinner, saying: "Enter ye in at the strait gate." Some ministers have not the gift of feeding the church of God and watering it. Paul planted—Apollos watered. Some are only door-keepers in the house of my God. Learn not to despise any of the true servants of God. Are all apostles? Are all prophets? He has appointed some to stand at the door, and some to break the children's bread—despise neither.

B. *All Christians are servants, and have their work assigned them.* Some people think that ministers only have to work for Christ; but see here: "He gave to every man his work." In a great house, the steward and the porter are not the only servants; there are many more, and all have their work to do. Just so among the people of Christ. Ministers are not the only servants of Christ; all that believe on Him are His servants.

(1.) Learn to be working Christians. "Be ye doers of the Word, and not hearers only, deceiving your own souls." It is very striking to see the uselessness of many Christians. Are there none of you who know what it is to be selfish in your Christianity? You have seen a selfish child go into a secret place to enjoy some delicious morsels undisturbed by his companions? So it is with some Christians. They feed upon Christ and forgiveness; but it is alone, and all for themselves. Are there not some of you who can enjoy being a Christian, while your dearest friend is not; and yet you will not speak to him? See here, you have got your work to do. When Christ found you, He said: "Go, work in my vineyard." What were you hired for, if it was not to work? What were you saved for, if it was not to spread salvation? What blessed for? Oh! my Christian friends! how little you live as if you were servants of Christ!—how much idle time and idle talk you have! This is not like a good servant. How many things you have to do for yourself!—how few for Christ and His people! This is not like a servant.

(2.) Learn to keep to your own work. In a great house every servant has his own peculiar work. One man is the porter to open the door; another is the steward to provide food for the family; a third has to clean the rooms; a fourth has to dress the food; a fifth has to wait upon the guests. Everyone has his proper place, and no servant interferes with another. If all were to become porters, and open the door, then what would become of the stewardship? or, if all were to be stewards, who would clean the house? Just so is it with Christians. Everyone has his peculiar work assigned him, and should not leave it. "Let every man abide in the same calling wherein he was called." Obadiah had his work appointed him in the court of the wicked Ahab. God placed him as His servant there, saying: "Work here for me." Does any of you belong to a wicked family? Seek not to be removed—Christ has placed you there to be His servant—work for Him. The Shunammite had her work. When the prophet asked: "Wilt thou be spoken for to the king?" she said: "I dwell among mine own people." Once a poor demoniac whom Jesus healed, besought Jesus that he might follow after Him; howbeit Jesus suffered him not, but saith unto him: "Go home to thy friends, and tell them how great things the Lord hath done for thee, and how he hath had compassion on thee." Learn, my dear friends, to keep to your own work. When the Lord has hung up a lamp in one corner, is there no presumption in removing it to another? Is not the Lord wiser than man? Everyone of you have your work to do for Christ *where you are*. Are you on a sick-bed? Still you have your work to do for Christ there as much as the highest servant of Christ in the world. The smallest twinkling star is as much a servant of God as the mid-day sun. Only live for Christ where you are.

IV. *Christ is coming back again, and we know not when*: "Watch ye therefore: for ye know not when the master of the house cometh, at even, or at midnight, or at the cock-crowing, or in the morning: lest, coming suddenly, he find you sleeping" (vv. 35,36). Two things are here declared.

A. *That Christ is coming back again*. The whole Bible bears witness to this. The master of the house has been a long time away on His journey; but He will come back again. When Christ ascended from His disciples, and a cloud received Him out of their sight, and they were looking steadfastly into heaven, the angels said: "Ye men of Galilee, why stand ye gazing up into heaven? This same Jesus which is taken up form you into heaven, shall so come in like manner as ye have seen him go into heaven."

B. *That Christ will come back suddenly*. The whole Bible bears witness to this. (1.) In one place it is compared to a snare which suddenly entraps the unwary wild beast: "As a snare shall it come on all them that dwell on the face of the whole earth." (2.) Again, to a thief: "The day of the Lord so cometh as a thief in the night." (3.) Again, to a bridegroom coming suddenly: "At midnight there was a cry made, Behold the bridegroom cometh." (4.) Again, to the waters of the flood. (5.) Again, to the fiery rain that fell on Sodom and Gomorrah. (6.) And here to the sudden coming home of the master of the house: "Ye know not when the master of the house cometh." Now, my dear friends, I am far from discouraging those who, with humble prayerfulness, search into the records of prophecy to find out what God has said as to the second coming of the Son of Man. We are not like the first disciples of Jesus, if we do not often put the question: "What shall be the sign of thy coming, and of the end of the world?" But the truth which I wish to be written on your hearts is this: That the coming shall be sudden—sudden to the world—sudden to the children of God: "In such an hour as ye think not, the Son of Man cometh." "Ye know not when the master of the house cometh, at even, or at midnight, or at cockcrowing, or in the morning." Oh, my friends! your faith is incomplete, if you do not live in the daily faith of a coming Savior.

V. *Watch*: "And what I say unto you I say unto all, Watch" (v. 37).

A. *Ministers should watch.* This word is especially addressed to the porter: "Watch ye, therefore." Ah! how watchful we should be. Many things make up sleep. (1.) Want of faith. When a minister loses sight of Christ crucified—risen—coming again—then he cannot watch for souls. Pray that your ministers may have a watching eye always on Christ. (2.) Seeing so many careless souls. Ah! you little know how this staggers the ministers of Christ. A young believer comes with a glowing heart to tell of Christ, and pardon, and the new heart. He knows it is the truth of God—he states it simply, freely, with all his heart—he presses it on men—he hopes to see them melt like icicles before the sun—alas! they are as cold and dead as ever. They live on in their sins—they die in their sins. Ah! you little know how this makes him dull, and heavy, and heart-broken. My friends, pray that we may not sleep. Pray that your carelessness may only make us watch the more.

B. *Christians should watch.* Ah! if Christ is at hand, (1.) Take heed lest you be found unforgiven. Many Christians seem to live without a realizing view of Christ. The eye should be fixed on Christ. Your eye is shut. Oh! if you would abide in Christ, then let Him come tonight—at even, or at midnight, or at cockcrow, or in the morning—He is welcome, thrice welcome! Even so, come, Lord Jesus. (B.) Take heed lest you be found in any course of sin. Many Christians seem to walk, if I mistake not, in courses of sin. It is hard to account for it; but so it seems to be. Some Christians seem to be sleeping—in luxury—in covetousness—in evil company. Ah! think how would you like to be overtaken thus by the coming Savior. Try your daily occupations—your daily state of feeling—your daily enjoyments—try them by this test: Am I doing as I would wish to do on the day of His coming?

C. *Christless souls, how dreadful is your case*! Death may be sudden—oh! how awfully sudden it sometimes is. You may have no time for repentance—no breath to pray! The coming of the Savior shall be more sudden still. Ye know neither the day nor the hour. You know not God—you have not obeyed the Gospel. Oh! what will ye do in the day of the Lord's anger?

## Manifestation

**Henry ("Harry") Allan Ironside** (1878-1951) was born in Toronto, Canada, raised in California, and began preaching when he was converted at the age of fourteen. He had no formal training for the ministry but devoted himself to reading and studying of the Bible. His early associations were with the Salvation Army, but then he identified with the Plymouth Brethren and became one of their most beloved itinerant Bible teachers. From 1930 to 1948, he pastored the Moody Church in Chicago. He wrote more than sixty books, many of which are collections of messages given at Moody Church and various conferences.

This message is from *Great Words of the Gospel,* a series of messages given at Moody Church and published by Moody Press in 1944.

**Henry ("Harry") Allan Ironside**

# 6
# MANIFESTATION

I AM GOING TO ASK your attention to the fifth chapter of the second Epistle to the Corinthians, verses 9 and 10:

Wherefore we labor, that, whether present or absent, we may be accepted of him. For we must all appear before the judgment seat of Christ; that every one may receive the things done in his body, according to that he hath done, whether it be good or bad.

The second clause might be translated, "We must all be manifested before the judgment seat of Christ," and that is what I ask you to consider: the word "manifestation."

It will be a wonderful day when those who know the Lord and love Him shall appear in His presence, and when He will go back with us over all the path we have come since His grace has saved us. He will point out everything in our lives and service that has been in accordance with His own holy Word, everything that has been the result of the working of the Holy Spirit within us, and for all of that there will be a special reward in that day. He will also manifest all the selfishness, all the carelessness, all the worldliness, the lack of spirituality that has characterized many of us. He will show how we have missed our opportunities; how we could have been more faithful; how we could have been more devoted. But we were indifferent to the call of the Spirit of God, and because of all this we will suffer loss in that day.

I want you to notice several Scriptures that bring this thought before us, looking first at verse 9 which we have already read:

Wherefore we labor, that, whether present or absent, we may be accepted of him.

"Wherefore we labor," we make it our aim, we are ambitious, we have a laudable ambition, as we are going on in this scene for Christ. And what is that laudable ambition? That whether we remain in the body, or whether we go home to be with the Lord—for that is what is involved in the expression, "whether present or absent"—we will be well-pleasing unto Him.

### Accepted of Him

Do not confound this statement with a very similar expression in Ephesians 1:6, which has an altogether different meaning. There we read, "He," that is, God "hath made us," we who believe, "accepted in the beloved." Now that is true of every Christian. It is true of you who not very long ago were still walking in the world, with the worldlings, had not yet received Christ; but now you have trusted Him. The moment you put your trust in the Lord Jesus, God made you accepted in the Beloved. That is, God received you at that moment according to all the value that He put upon the person and work of His Son. What a wonderful thing that is! Accepted in Him!

What does it mean? It just means this: that the believer is as dear to the heart of the Father as the Lord Jesus is; that God thinks as much of you who have trusted Christ as He does of His own blessed Son. That may seem hard to believe; in fact, I could not believe it if I did not find it in my Bible, but I do find it there. In John 17, I hear the Lord Jesus praying to the Father and He uses this language: "That the world may know that thou hast sent me, and hast loved them, as thou hast loved me" (v. 23). Those are the Savior's own words. He says of every believer, of every child of God through faith in His name, of everyone of them, no matter what their experience may have been: "Thou hast loved them, as thou hast loved me."

There is another verse in the first Epistle of John that is very striking. It says there, "As he is," that is, as Christ is, "so are we in this world" (4:17). I remember years ago when I just could not take that in. I would read those words, "As he is, so are we in this world," and I would say to myself, "Oh no, not I! I am not as holy, I am not as compassionate, I am not as much concerned about lost sinners as He is." I could not say that I am as He is right down here in this world. I felt as though I could have understood it better if it had said, "As he is, so *shall* we be when we leave this world," for I confidently hoped to become some day exactly like Him; but to say, "As he is, so *are* we in this world," that was altogether too much for me in those days. I felt that I could have understood if He had said, "As he is, so *ought* we to be in this world," because I felt it was my duty to be as much like Him as possible in this world. But the definite statement that, "As he is, so *are* we in this world" was more than I could take in, until light from heaven shone upon this passage and I saw that what He was speaking about was not exactly our personal experience, or our personal growth in grace, or our likeness to Christ in that way; but it was our justification before God, our acceptance in the Beloved. In that sense, God sees every believer in Christ. As He is, so are we before God down here in this world.

That is what is involved in the Epistle to the Romans, chapter 8: "There is therefore now no condemnation to them which are in Christ Jesus." I am in Him before the Father. He sees me in His Son and I have a perfect, a complete standing in Christ. Every believer is made meet to be a partaker "of the inheritance of the saints in light."

But now in verse 9 of Second Corinthians, chapter 5, the apostle says, "Wherefore we labor, that, whether present or absent, we may be accepted of him." Notice "accepted of him," not accepted *in* him. "Accepted of him" means well pleasing to Him. Now he is referring to our behavior, to our practical experience, to our service; and he says, "We are laboring, we are working now, we are ambitious to be well-pleasing to Him. We want his approbation day by day." I want the approval of the Lord; don't you? I can hardly conceive of a Christian who does not desire that his life be pleasing to God.

## Appearing before Him

And then he goes on to say, "For we must all appear," we must all be manifested, "before the judgment seat of Christ." The day is coming when we are going to leave this scene. The Lord is coming back for His own, and the dead shall be raised and the living changed. Then we shall appear at His judgment seat. Somebody may say, "How do you know that this judgment seat of Christ is just subsequent to the rapture of the Church?" Well, in the book of the Revelation, the last chapter, we get this: "Behold, I come quickly; and my reward is with me, to give every man according as his work shall be" (22:12). You see, when He comes again, when He returns for His own, His reward will be with Him. The judgment seat of Christ is the place where we shall be manifested in order that we may receive our reward. And so the apostle says, "We must all," we believers—he is speaking of the two classes, the resurrected dead and the living who shall be changed—"We must all appear before the judgment seat of Christ."

Somebody has suggested that the original word here has really the thought of a complete opening up, a complete unveiling, and it might be translated, "We shall all be turned inside out at the judgment seat of Christ." How would you like to be turned inside out now? How would you like to have all your thoughts made manifest? all your hidden motives? I think that would be rather humbling for some of us.

There is more hypocrisy about many of us than we would like to let people know. Of course, if people knew, then it would no longer be hypocrisy. We may do some covering up now, but the day is coming when it will all be made manifest. One may pretend to be humble and lowly and to seek the will of the Lord, and all the time in the heart there is envy and strife and jealousy of others, and one does not like to see other people recognized in place of oneself.

Oh, if we were turned inside out now, I think there would be some tremendous showings up! Friends would see a lot of things that many of them never dreamed were hidden away in the heart. Well, we ought to be real, we ought to seek to be genuine, because it is all coming out some day. The Lord Jesus has told us that everything is going to be made manifest in that coming day. Every idle word and the thoughts of the heart are going to be made known. "We must all be made manifest before the judgment seat of Christ."

And let me say this. The judgment seat of Christ, as we have it here, should not be confounded with the judgment of the great white throne at the end of the world. Now, of course, the great white throne will be Christ's judgment seat also. He said, "The Father judgeth no man, but hath committed all judgment unto the Son" (John 5:22). So when the wicked dead are raised at the end of time and they stand before the great white throne, do you know who will be seated on that throne? The same blessed One who suffered once to save them, and from whom they have turned away. They will behold seated on the throne of judgment the Man who hung on Calvary's cross, the Lord Jesus Christ, for He is God as well as Man. God is going to judge the world, but He is going to judge the world in the person of His Son.

The judgment of the great white throne, of which we read in Revelation 20, is the judgment of the wicked. The judgment seat of Christ is a different type of judgment altogether. It is the judgment of God's beloved people when they come before Him to give an account of their lives since He saved them. They are not going there to be judged for their sins, because these have all been put away by the precious blood of Christ; but they are going there to give an account of their service, and the Lord will take cognizance of all that His people have done, whether it has been good or bad, whether it has been the work of the flesh or the work of the Spirit: "that every one may receive the things done in his body, according to that he hath done, whether it be good or bad" (2 Cor. 5:10).

It will be a very wonderful time when we stand there in our glorified bodies. You see, we will not go there to find out whether we are going to heaven, but we will be there glorified in our resurrection bodies. It will be a very wonderful time when we stand there before our blessed Lord and He says, "Now I am going to show you how all of your works appeared to me." To many of us it will be a tremendous revelation. We have worked hard and labored long, and sometimes we have been so discouraged and felt as though we had not accomplished anything; and then the Lord is going to open things up and say, "You remember the time when you were so disheartened? You just felt that you were working away and your ministry wasn't counting for anything, but at that very time this precious soul was brought to know Christ." That night when you were so discouraged and you felt that you were such a failure as a preacher, and you told the Lord that perhaps you didn't belong in the ministry at all, you will find at the judgment seat of Christ that the Lord used that message to lead some soul to Himself.

We have those experiences here on earth sometimes. I remember one time I had prayed so earnestly for a meeting, and I spent so much time before God and my expectation was great. I just poured my heart out in the message that night, but there was no response at all. Nobody seemed to be interested, and I did not even try to get down to the door to meet anybody, I felt so discouraged. So I slipped out the back way and went home and threw myself down on my knees and cried out to the Lord, telling Him what a complete failure I was and that nobody got any blessing. I was so utterly disheartened! Then about three months later I was leaving that place after having worked on for nine months in all, and I got a letter from a young woman who had been singing in the choir.

She wrote me and said, "I have never told you of my salvation, and I feel that before you go I ought to tell you." She gave me the exact date. She said it was so vivid in her mind that she would never forget it. "I was singing in the choir that night. In fact," she said, "I sang a solo. You know, I always thought I was a Christian, but that night God revealed my own heart to me. I saw that I had never been converted, and when you asked for anybody who wanted to receive Christ to come to Him then, I had such an urge to walk down to the platform and publicly confess Christ, but I was ashamed. I went home so miserable, so wretched; but thank God, before I retired I broke down before Him. I got down on my knees and confessed my sins and took Christ as my Savior, and everything has been so different since. I have never had the courage to tell you before, but I felt that I must tell you before you left."

I checked up and found that it was that night when I was so utterly discouraged. That night God had wrought a miracle in that young woman's life.

I think there will be many things like that in the day of manifestation. I think the Lord will show many of us how He used the Word, when we did not know He was using it at all. Or just the manner of life lived will have borne fruit in someone's life, and at the judgment seat of Christ that one will say, "I watched that man, that woman, at their work; I watched them when things went wrong, and they manifested such a kind, gracious spirit. I watched to see if they would get angry or upset when their wishes were crossed, but they were so meek and so gracious and so Christianlike. I said to myself, 'There is something there I would give a great deal to have.' That message led me to Christ. I have never told them, but I am telling them now."

## Rewarded by Him

Many things are going to come out like that, and for everything that has been done for Christ, there will be rewards. But there will be the other side of it. I am afraid many of us will be disappointed in that day. So much of our service has been done in the energy of the flesh, and we shall be disappointed when the Lord has to say to us, "Your life hasn't counted very much for me. You were so much concerned with magnifying yourself, with building up your own reputation, with what people would think of you, and you just fattened on applause and praise. Well, you have had your reward. I do not have any for you now. You had it all down there. You will have to suffer loss. You did not work for My glory; you were not concerned about making me known. You were concerned about your own reputation. You wanted people to speak well of you. Well, you have had your success, but there is no reward for you here."

> He is coming! Oh, how solemn!
> When the Judge's voice is heard,
> And in His own light He shows us
> Every thought and act and word!

Deeds of merit, as we thought them,
He will show us were but sin;
Little acts we had forgotten,
He will tell us were for Him.

It will be a wonderful thing to get His mind about it all, but a very solemn thing, too.

Now turn back to that passage in the first Epistle to the Corinthians, chapter 3. These Corinthians were making a great deal of Christian leaders, so much so that they were actually dividing themselves, sectarianly. One of them would say, "I am of Paul," another would say, "I am of Apollos," and still another would say, "I am of Cephas." I don't know that they used the actual names. I really don't think they did, because the sixth verse of the fourth chapter, it seems to me, negatives that:

"And these things, brethren, I have in a figure transferred to myself and to Apollos for your sakes; that ye might learn in us not to think of men above that which is written, that no one of you be puffed up for one against another. For who maketh thee to differ from another? and what hast thou that thou didst not receive? now if thou didst receive it, why dost thou glory, as if thou hadst not received it?" (1 Cor. 4:6,7).

You see, "I have transferred these things in a figure to myself and to Apollos." What probably was taking place was this:

Some were saying, "I enjoy a man like Paul who really teaches the Word. I do not care to go and hear these lightweights. I like a man who digs down under the letter and gives us something weighty." Another says, "I haven't much use for that dry as dust Bible teacher. He is too deep for me. I like a man who can soar up into the clouds. I enjoy one who can preach with unction and liberty, an eloquent man, and a man mighty in the Scriptures. Give me Apollos! I like to hear a great preacher. I am not interested in going to church when somebody is just expounding the Bible. I want something that thrills me." Another says, "I like the exhorter. I like the man who gets down to something practical and stirs you up, and makes you feel your own need and the importance of Christian living. I am not interested in Bible teaching or in eloquent preaching. I like good, faithful exhortation. I am of Cephas."

But the apostle says, "They have all received their gifts of the Lord, and the gifts are for the whole Church. Do not under-value one and put the other on a pedestal. Thank God for them all. There are some times when you need the Bible teacher; there are times when you need the eloquent preacher; and there are times when you need the exhorter. Thank God for every one of them." See what he says:

"Who then is Paul, and who is Apollos, but ministers by whom ye believed, even as the Lord gave to every man? I have planted, Apollos watered; but God gave the increase. So then neither is he that planteth any thing, neither he that watereth; but God that giveth the increase" (1 Cor. 3:5-7).

In other words, don't make too much of the instrument. It is God who gives the increase, and whether He works through the teacher or the preacher or the exhorter, you just give Him the glory; give Him the praise.

Then as to the laborer, "He that planteth and he that watereth are one," and he has already said that they are both nothing; so they are just men, both of them. They do not amount to anything in themselves, but "every man shall receive his own reward according to his own labor" (v. 8). There you have it! That is the reward that Christians are to receive at the judgment seat of Christ. You do your work faithfully in the place that God has put you and do not be worried because you cannot do what someone else is doing. You will get your reward. There is no need to be jealous; there is no need to be envious because someone else gets more recognition than you do. Do that which God has commanded you, and do it as unto the Lord. Each shall receive his own reward according to his own labor.

"Ye are God's husbandry, ye are God's building. According to the grace of God which is given unto me, as a wise master-builder . . ." (1 Cor. 3:9,10).

Paul had gone into Corinth and laid out the plans for the work, and was used of God to establish the church there.

"I have laid the foundation, and another buildeth thereupon. But let every man take heed how he buildeth thereupon. For other foundation can no man lay than that is laid, which is Jesus Christ" (vv. 10,11).

The Church rests upon Christ, and Christ alone.

"Now if any man build upon this foundation"—he is on the Foundation; he in in Christ. Now he is building: "Gold, silver, precious stones. . . ." These will glorify God. They speak of that which is precious in His sight.

But then there are "wood, hay, stubble." These speak of that which is worthless; they will never abide the test of judgment fire.

"Every man's work shall be make manifest." This tells us that everything will come out in that day:

"For the day shall declare it, because it shall be revealed by fire."

The fire of God's holiness will test every man's work. Will it come up to God's standard? Will it come up to what He has a right to expect? He is going to test it! "The fire shall try every man's work of what sort it is."

It is a great comfort to me to know that it does not say, "How *much* it is." All my life there has been so much I have wanted to do; there have been so many, many places I should like to go and preach; there are so many things I wish I could accomplish for Christ, but time and strength make it impossible. As I look back over the years, I have been able to do so little compared with what I might have done; but I get a lot of comfort out of this Scripture: "Every man's work shall be made manifest: for the day shall declare it, because it shall be revealed by fire; and the fire shall try every man's work of *what sort* it is." And my heart says. "O Lord, help me to do the right sort of work, even if I can't do a great deal. God give me to do the right sort—the work that is the result of the control of the Holy Spirit in my life, in accordance with the Word of God."

"If any man's work abide which he hath built thereupon, he shall receive a reward" (v. 14).

This is not salvation; this is reward! You say, "Well, do you work for a reward?" We work for the glory of God, but He delights to give rewards.

I attended a men's banquet at one of our city churches one night, where I was to speak, and they had just been doing a good deal of building and in a very nice way they were recognizing the different men who had accomplished quite a little in their program. One dear aged brother was called to the front, and they said something like this: "He has probably done more for the work of the church on this occasion than almost anyone else," and they wanted to give him a gift. He came forward quite diffidently and said, "What I did, I did for the Lord. I was not looking for any thanks and I was not looking for any gift, but since you have been so kind and have done this for me, I accept your gift and thank you for it."

I think that is the way we will speak to the Lord when He says, "Now, you did this for me, and you did that and you did the other, and now I want to reward you. I am going to give you a crown of righteousness, or a crown of glory." I think we shall feel like saying, "Blessed Lord, I did not do that for a reward; I did it for Thee because I love Thee. But since in Thy rich grace Thou delightest to give rewards. I receive it as from Thyself and thank Thee for it."

In the day of manifestation! And I think we shall feel ashamed, if we have nothing for which we may be rewarded.

"If any man's work shall be burned (if all his work seems to go for nothing), he shall suffer loss" (v. 15).

This will have nothing to do with the question of his eternal salvation, for we read:

"But he himself shall be saved; yet so as by fire."

God grant that each one of us may serve faithfully in view of that day of manifestation, and that we may have a rich reward because of heart devotion to Christ down here!

## The Relationship of the Doctrine of the Return of Christ to Practical Holiness

**William Culbertson** (1905-1971) was born and educated in Philadelphia and was identified all of his ministry with the Reformed Episcopal Church of America. He pastored churches in Pennsylvania and New Jersey and in 1937 was elected Bishop of the New York and Philadelphia Synod. In 1942, he became Dean of Education at the Moody Bible Institute in Chicago; and in 1947 was named Acting President upon the death of Will H. Houghton. In 1948, he became president of the school, a position he held with distinction until 1971, when he was named Chancellor. "My first impression and the lasting one," said Dr. Wilbur M. Smith, "is that he is a man of God." He was in great demand as a preacher and widely recognized as a leader in Christian education.

This sermon comes from the compilation of his Moody Bible Institute "Founder's Week" messages *The Faith Once Delivered*, published in 1972 by Moody Press, and is used by permission.

William Culbertson

# 7

## THE RELATIONSHIP OF THE DOCTRINE OF THE RETURN OF CHRIST TO PRACTICAL HOLINESS

Colossians 3

MAY I AT THE OUTSET affirm that here at Moody Bible Institute we continue our belief in the fact of the second advent, and that it is premillennial and imminent; and further, that we look for our Lord's coming for His own to precede the tribulation. However, these matters, as important as they are, are not the object of our consideration now.

There is another important consideration connected with holiness which will not be involved in our development of the subject today, namely, the completion and the perfection of God's redemptive process as it relates to the believer's soul and body. This final perfecting of believers in the image and likeness of their Lord is necessary to the honesty and the integrity of the Bible's teaching concerning holiness. Without our Lord's return, the perfection of the believer is not attained, for it is when we see Him that we shall be like Him. Without the perfection of the believer, what about the plan of God, what about the efficacy of the atonement, what about the honesty of the biblical ethic which demands perfection?

Perfection is to be realized by you and me, and that realization is fully accomplished at the return of our Lord. That is an important consideration, and shows the imperative necessity of an eschatology which involves the return of the Lord Jesus Christ.

But pass from such matters to the relationship of this doctrine to practical holiness. We, of course, are thankful to God for our perfect standing before Him in our Lord and Savior Jesus Christ. But what is true judicially and positionally is one thing; what our practice is, what our state is, may be quite another thing. We have position. What about condition? We know Christ's headship. What about fellowship? Our concern, therefore, is the relationship of the doctrine of the return of our Lord and Savior to practice holiness—our spiritual condition, our spiritual fellowship with God now.

As I study the Word of God is seems to me that the meaning of this subject upon practical holiness may be seen in two lines of teaching. The first line of teaching brings several Scriptures before us which show the relationship of the truth of our Lord's return to specific items of behavior. In other words, the coming of our Lord is specifically associated with our conduct in particular. Four areas of behavior are definitely linked with the doctrine of the return of our Lord and Savior Jesus Christ.

The second line of teaching is more general and shows how the doctrine of the return of our Lord affects the motivation of believers. After all, we need some sure spring of action. We need some influence, some incentive, some stimulus to right conduct. And this hope of the coming of the Lord furnishes such prompting, such inspiration, such drive.

## Its Effects on Conduct

First of all, then, we want to look at what the Scriptures have to say about the effects of the doctrine of the return of our Lord upon certain specific items of conduct. Turn in your Bible with me to Colossians 3.

Colossians 3:4 says: "When Christ, who is our life, shall be manifested, then shall ye also with him be manifested in glory." Now this verse is referring to the return of our Lord; He is to be manifested. The verse actually is part of a fuller text which has to do with our Lord's resurrection, His ascension, and His present ministry in heaven. So, in chronological sequence, the next item to come before us in such a listing of events is the return of the Lord Jesus.

Says the Scripture: "Set your mind on the things that are above, not on the things that are upon the earth. For ye died, and your life is his with Christ in God. When Christ, who is our life, shall be manifested [He is coming again; He will appear] then shall ye also with him be manifested in glory" (vv. 2-4). And so our minds and our hearts are directed toward the truth of the coming again of the Lord Jesus.

Now what follows? "Put to death therefore your members which are upon the earth" (v. 5). "Therefore"—because these facts are true, that Christ arose, that Christ ascended, that Christ is seated in the heavens, that Christ is coming again, and that you are united with Him in each of these historic facts—His resurrection, His ascension, His being seated in the heavenlies, His return—since this is true, "put to death your members which are upon the earth."

The apostle goes on to name some of the deeds done by our members which are upon the earth. "Fornication, uncleanness, passion, evil desire, and covetousness" are all to be put away.

Thus you see the return of our Lord, along with the other doctrines to which we have alluded, has a definite bearing and a definite relationship to our moral living now. In other words, we are not to commit fornication, we are not to be characterized by uncleanness, passion, evil desire and covetousness. Why? Because the Lord is coming again.

I hardly think it is necessary for me to develop all that is involved in these things which are listed for us here. Fornication is illicit sexual intercourse. Uncleanness has to do with profligate living. Passion has to do with ungovernable desire, evil desire, the cravings of the old nature, the flesh. Covetousness, which is particularly singled out and emphasized in this listing, has to do with the greedy desire to have more. These sins are not to be characteristic of the child of God; he believes the Lord is coming again. Therefore he is to put away, to put to death, these things.

If you go on and read the following verses, anger, wrath, malice, railing, shameful speaking and lying are all specifically mentioned. Thus, here in this text we have set before us the fact that there is a relationship in God's Word between the truth of the manifestation of the Son of God in His second coming, and the moral living on the part of the child of God now.

Look at the second passage. In 1 Corinthians 4 the Word of God associates the coming of our Lord with hasty and uncharitable criticism. "With me it is a very small thing that I should be judged of you, or of man's day: yea, I judge not mine own self. For I know nothing against myself; yet am I not hereby justified: but he that judgeth me is the Lord. Wherefore judge nothing before the time, until the Lord come, who will both bring to light the hidden things of darkness, and make manifest the counsels of the hearts; and then shall each man have his praise from God" (1 Cor. 4:3-5, margin).

### Its Effect on Perspective

I recognize that the child of God must make certain tests. A certain amount of judgment—I trust spiritually engaged in according to the teaching of the Word of God—must characterize the faithful child of God. He must distinguish between the true and the false. He must be in a position to condemn error and sin and commend truth and righteousness. So I am not among those who deprecate all kinds of judgment. But it is entirely possible that our judgment will be formed too hastily and will be entered into quite uncharitably—and these things are wrong.

Paul is telling us here that it is well to wait until the coming of the Lord with regard to certain judgments; thus we shall be delivered from the sin of unjust and uncharitable judgment. Our Lord will bring to light the hidden things of darkness. It is well for us to avoid harsh, hasty, unduly critical and uncharitable judgment.

I suppose we all, to greater or lesser extent, have been guilty of this kind of criticism on occasion. We see something and we add two and two together and we say it makes four—there can be no other answer. Therefore, we utterly condemn the individual who has been guilty of what we have seen. We have no way of knowing his motives, but we condemn him because his motives *must* be bad.

Incidentally, have you ever noticed—I say it to our shame—how quick we are to believe the worst about someone? God help us! Some idle word of gossip and our ears are alert and our minds are feverishly active. God help us! This passage of Scripture connects the fact that the Lord is coming again with an avoidance of harsh, hasty criticism.

Look at it again. Paul says, "It is a very small thing with me that I should be judged of you." I like that, don't you? I can't say I've always been able to live that way, but I like it. We get awfully bothered about what people think of us. And if the Lord should ask us to do something that people would misunderstand, we usually have an argument with the Lord that we shouldn't do it because we like to be thought of favorably. But Paul says, "It is a very small thing that I should be judged of you, or of man's day"—man's day meaning the judgments, the norms, the standards adopted by men. "It is a small thing that I should be judged by them just because I don't fit their worldly pattern. That doesn't bother me a bit." It oughtn't bother us.

"It is a very small thing that I should be judged of you, or of man's day: yea, I judge not mine own self." Does that mean Paul never looked inward to discover whether or not he was truly obedient to God? I don't think it means that. I think it means that he didn't judge so as to commend himself in pride. Paul says, "I know nothing against myself: yet am I not hereby justified." Paul understood—and God helped us to understand—that there are secrets in the innermost recesses of our hearts that even we ourselves are not fully conscious of. Just because I know nothing against myself, I am not thereby justified. He that judgeth me is the Lord, and when the Lord comes, He's going to judge.

Now notice verse 5 says He will "bring to light the hidden things of darkness, and make manifest the counsels of the hearts." I view that statement with mingled emotions. In one sense I am glad, in another sense I am in great trepidation. I'm glad because I know that when I have done something wrong, but out of pure motives, God will understand that, and certainly some allowance will be made. I have said I would do something, I thought I could, but circumstances have come about making it impossible, and I'm embarrassed. I meant to do it; my motives were pure. God knows my motives—you don't, and I don't know yours. But this verse says that it will be brought to light. I'm glad for that, because I'm sure I've offended some of my best friends and some whom I love deeply just because they didn't know my motives; they have seen only my clumsy, faltering deeds. They could only see what happened, they didn't know what was really in my heart.

But then, in a little measure, I do know what is in my heart, and with mortal shame I have to look back on those circumstances when I did things for which men have praised me but I have had wrong motives, and they're going to be brought to light too. Is it any wonder that there are trepidation and fear?

There are two things I want to say. Thank God for the blood of the Lord Jesus. I would not want to live if I didn't have the assurance in my soul that the blood of Jesus Christ, God's Son, cleanseth us from all sin.

But a second thing I want to say stirs my soul and lifts me to the heights! "And then shall each man have his praise from God." It doesn't say, "And then shall each man be censured by God." It could have said that. However little I have to offer, my blessed heavenly Father and my dear Savior are going to find something for which to give praise. Oh, the wonderful, wonderful grace of God!

You see, in this second passage of Scripture the coming of the Lord is related to a specific item of conduct, a definite act of behavior which has to do with hasty and uncharitable judgment.

Look at a third passage. In 2 Timothy 4:8 we read: "Henceforth there is laid up for me the crown of righteousness, which the Lord, the righteous judge, shall give to me at that day; and not to me only, but also to all them that have loved his appearing."

For what is this crown of righteousness given when the Lord comes again at that day? Paul says, "I have fought the good fight, I have finished the course, I have kept the faith: henceforth there is laid up for me the crowns of righteousness" (vv. 7-8). The crown of righteousness is reward for faithfulness in ministry. Paul fought the good fight, he finished the course, he kept the faith. That's why there is a crown of righteousness of which he could talk. It will be his when the Lord Jesus comes again.

You say, "Wait a minute, that's well and good, but don't you see that so far as the rest of us are concerned, there's another reason why this crown of righteousness is ours?" Paul does add at the end of verse 8, "and not to me only, but also to all them that have loved his appearing." So you affirm: "Paul had to fight the good fight, he had to finish the course, he had to keep the faith; but all we have to do is love His appearing!" You poor, miserable, unspiritual, carnal Christian. Do you think that's what this verse means? Do you think when some lovely emotion that I in ecstasy have about the coming of the Lord thrills my soul, that means I'm going to get the crown of righteousness? You're wrong, you're wrong! You'll get the crown of righteousness on the same basis Paul gets it, or you won't get it at all.

### Its Effect on Attitude

Invariably, in the Word of God loving the appearing of Christ is associated with faithful ministry to the one whose appearing you love. If you say you love the appearing of Christ and are indifferent to the claims of Christ and are unspiritual in your living and are worldly and careless in your life, there is no crown of righteousness waiting for you. You don't truly love His appearing. So let's define the term correctly.

Once again, do you see that the apostle is talking about the return of Christ? It is at the return of Christ that the rewards are distributed. That coming should have a relationship to how I live now.

Look at a fourth passage of Scripture in 1 Thessalonians 3:12-13: "and the Lord make you to increase and about in love one toward another, and toward all men, even as we also do toward you; to the end he may establish your hearts unblamable in holiness before our God and Father, at the coming of our Lord Jesus with all his saints." What is the specific items of conduct singled out here for our attention and related to the coming of our Lord? Brotherly love. Here is a subject about which we all can talk, but about which we all need to learn so much more than we know.

I'm not pleading for a weak, emaciated, superficial kind of affection. I know that true love always involves faithfulness and integrity. But, even so, we have fallen far short in the matter of brotherly love, of sympathy, of concern, of care, of a willingness to go out of our way to help our brother, to help all men.

So if the hope of the return of our Lord is held by us, it should affect our personal behavior in these four areas of life: morality, judgment, service and love.

In the Word of God the doctrine of the return of our Lord Jesus Christ has a bearing not only on the particular outward manifestation of our life and conduct, but it reaches into the inner being and has to do with the motivation of our life. Let me briefly mention four areas.

The second coming of our Lord Jesus Christ in the Word of God has an appeal to our sense of urgency. Our motivation is accelerated because we know that the Lord may come. I am forced to action if I believe He's coming. I am speaking here particularly of the imminency of His coming. However the term "imminency" is defined, I find that by far the largest group of evangelical Christians whom I know, whatever their eschatological view, is looking for the return of the Lord Jesus Christ. And that's what I'm talking about here; let's not argue at this point.

What was it the Lord Jesus said? "Watch therefore: for ye know not on what day your Lord cometh." Immediately following that utterance of our Lord there is recorded this additional word: "But know this, that if the master of the house had known in what watch the thief was coming, he would have watched, and would not have suffered his house to be broken through. Therefore be ye also ready; for in an hour that ye think not the Son of man cometh" (Matt. 24:42-44). Urgency! We have a task to perform. Let us be up and doing. Said our Lord, "The night cometh when no man can work." No wonder our gospel hymn sounds the refrain:

> Work, for the night is coming,
> Work through the morning hours;
> Work while the dew is sparkling,
> Work, mid springing flowers;
> Work when the day grows brighter,
> Work in the glowing sun;
> Work, for the night is coming.
> When man's work is done.
> —Annie L. Walker

I like the paraphrase of that gospel hymn which has come to us anonymously and reads like this:

> Work, then, the Day is coming!
> No time for sighing now!
> Harps for the hands once cropping,
> Wreaths for the victor's brow.
> Now morning Light is breaking,
> Soon will the Day appear;
> Night shades appall no longer,
> Jesus Christ is near.

The doctrine of the return of the Lord strikes another chord in motivation in its appeal to the sense of values. You recall how the apostle Peter develops this theme in 2 Peter 3:10-14: "But the day of the Lord will come as a thief; in the which the heavens shall pass away with a great noise, and the elements shall be dissolved with fervent heat, and the earth and the works that are therein shall be burned up. Seeing that these things are thus all to be dissolved, what manner of persons ought ye to be in all holy living and godliness, looking for and earnestly desiring the coming of the day of God, by reason of which the heavens being on fire shall be dissolved, and the elements shall melt with fervent heat? But, according to his promise, we look for new heavens and a new earth, wherein dwelleth righteousness. Wherefore, beloved, seeing that ye look for these things, give diligence that ye may be found in peace, without spot and blameless in his sight."

The truth of the coming of the Lord Jesus Christ and the associated events connected therewith in the end times are laid hold of by Peter and, led of the Holy Spirit, he says, "What manner of persons ought ye to be in all holy living and godliness?" Because the things of time and sense are all going to pass away.

For what are you living? Said the apostle Paul, the things which are seen are temporal, but the things which are not seen are eternal. Said the Lord Jesus, "Lay up for yourselves treasures in heaven, where neither moth nor rust doth consume, and where thieves do not break through nor steal" (Matt. 6:20).

The second coming of Christ urges upon us the choice of living for God as over against living for the things of time and sense. His coming—mark it well, child of God—ultimately means the dissolution of all that some people hold dear, for the heavens and the earth shall be dissolved; and this world is all that some are living for. The doctrine of the return of Christ impinges upon our motivation by reminding us of a true sense of values, so our vision does not get distorted, our perspective is not out of line, and we understand things for what they are.

Please do not interpret what I am saying as meaning that we ought to be absolutely oblivious of the things of time and sense. My plea is to live for God down here and to utilize the things of time and sense for the honor and glory of God.

There's a third area of motivation, the appeal to the sense of duty, the matter of responsibility in the light of the return of the Lord Jesus. Says Revelation 22:12, "Behold, I come quickly; and my reward is with me, to render to each man according as his work is."

We can speak so glibly about the coming of our Lord and about the judgment seat of Christ! Have you ever taken your Bible and turned to one of these passages which speaks about the judgment of believers when our Lord comes again, and allowed the Spirit of God to burn into your soul some of the expressions involved? Let me give you one example of God's dealing with me.

In 2 Corinthians 5:10 I read: "We must all be made

manifest before the judgment seat of Christ." We *must.* There is no alternative; there is no other course. This rendering has special significance: "We must all be *made manifest.*" "All things are naked and laid opened before the eyes of him with whom we have to do" (Heb. 4:13). All things are stripped and stunned in the sight of Him with whom we have to do. We must appear at the judgment seat of Christ. We must be *made manifest* there.

Here is stress upon motivation. The Lord cometh! I must give an account for the deeds done in the body. I'm responsible. So I move out of my complacency, out of my easygoing ways; I have a duty to perform.

One thing more. The coming of our Lord in the Word of God is associated with the appeal to the sense of the disciple's loyalty, of the disciple's devotion and of the disciple's love.

Said the Lord Jesus: "If I go . . . I come again . . . that where I am, there ye may be also" (John 14:3). The apostle Paul speaks of loving His appearing (2 Tim. 4:8). My friend, if there is any holy emotion in your soul of dedication and loyalty and love to the Lord Jesus it is because He is coming again, the Bridegroom is coming! A proper understanding of what my attitude shall be toward Him who is the Lover of my soul means that I shall live for Him whom I love.

Thus the four areas of motivation affected by the doctrine of our Lord's return are urgency, a sense of values, a sense of duty, and a sense of loyalty and love. You do not truly hold the truth of the doctrine of the return of the Lord Jesus Christ until that doctrine holds you, and influences your manner of living as the Bible says it should.

## Christ's Advent to Judgment

**Jeremy Taylor** (1613-1667) was educated at Cambridge, became a Fellow of All Soul's College in Oxford, and from 1638 to 1642 served as rector of the church in Uppingham. During the Civil War, he remained true to the royalist cause and served as chaplain in ordinary to Charles I. Following the victory of Cromwell, Taylor went to Wales where he ministered for ten years and wrote some of his best-known works, including *Holy Living* and *Holy Dying*. From 1658 until his death, Taylor served in Ireland and eventually became Bishop of Down and Connor in Ulster.

The message is taken from *A Treasury of the World's Great Sermons* edited by Warren W. Wiersbe and published by Kregel Publications.

**Jeremy Taylor**

# 8

# CHRIST'S ADVENT TO JUDGMENT

> For we must all appear before the judgment seat of Christ, that everyone may receive the things done in his body, according to that he hath done, whether it be good or bad (2 Cor. 5:10).

IF WE CONSIDER the person of the Judge, we first perceive that He is interested in the injury of the crimes He is to sentence: "They shall look on Him whom they have pierced." It was for thy sins that the Judge did suffer such unspeakable pains as were enough to reconcile all the world to God; the sum and spirit of which pains could not be better understood than by the consequence of His own words, "My God, my God, why hast thou forsaken me?" meaning, that He felt such horrible, pure, unmingled sorrows, that, although His human nature was personally united to the Godhead, yet at that instant He felt no comfortable emanations by sensible perception from the Divinity, but He was so drenched in sorrow that the Godhead seemed to have forsaken Him. Beyond this, nothing can be added: but then, that thou hast for thy own particular made all this sin in vain and ineffective, that Christ thy Lord and Judge should be tormented for nothing, that thou wouldst not accept felicity and pardon when he purchased them at so dear a price, must needs be an infinite condemnation to such person. How shalt thou look upon Him that fainted and died for love of thee, and thou didst scorn His miraculous mercies? How shall we dare to behold that holy face that brought salvation to us, and we turned away and fell in love with death, and kissed deformity and sins? And yet in the beholding that face consists much of the glories of eternity.

## The Person of the Judge

All the pains and passions, the sorrows and the groans, the humility and poverty, the labors and watchings, the prayers and the sermons, the miracles and the prophecies, the whip and the nails, the death and the burial, the shame and the smart, the cross and the grave of Jesus, shall be laid upon thy score, if thou hast refused the mercies and design of all their holy ends and purposes. And if we remember what a calamity that was which broke the Jewish nation in pieces, when Christ came to judge them for their murdering Him who was their King and the Prince of Life, and consider that this was but a dark image of the terrors of the day of judgment, we may then apprehend that there is some strange unspeakable evil that attends them that are guilty of this death, and of so much evil to their Lord. Now it is certain if thou wilt not be saved by His death, you are guilty of His death; if thou wilt not suffer Him to have thee, thou art guilty of destroying Him; and then let it be considered what is to be expected from that Judge before whom you stand as His murderer and betrayer. But this is but half of this consideration.

Christ may be crucified again, and upon a new account, put to an open shame. For after that Christ has done all this by the direct actions of His priestly office, of sacrificing himself for us, He hath also done very many things for us which are also the fruits of His first love and prosecutions of our redemption. I will not instance the strange arts of mercy that our Lord uses to bring us to live holy lives; but I consider, that things are so ordered, and so great a value set upon our souls since they are the images of God, and redeemed by the blood of the Holy Lamb, that the salvation of our souls is reckoned as a part of of His humanity. Every sinner that repents causes joy to Christ, and the joy is so great that it runs over and wets the fair brows and beauteous looks of cherubim and seraphim, and all the angels have a part of that banquet; then it is that our blessed Lord feels the fruits of His holy death; the acceptation of His holy sacrifice, the graciousness of

His person, the return of His prayers. For all that Christ did or suffered, and all that He now does as a priest in heaven, is to glorify His Father by bringing souls to God. For this it was that He was born and died, that He descended from heaven to earth, from life to death, from the cross to the grave; this was the purpose of His resurrection and ascension, of the end and design of all the miracles and graces of God manifested to all the world by Him; and now what man is so vile, such a malicious fool, that will refuse to bring joy to his Lord by doing himself the greatest good in the world? They who refuse to do this, are said to crucify the Lord of Life again, and put Him to an open shame—that is, they, as much as in them lies, bring Christ from His glorious joys to the labors of His life and the shame of His death; they advance His enemies, and refuse to advance the kingdom of their Lord; they put themselves in that state in which they were when Christ came to die for them; and now that He is in a state that He may rejoice over them (for He hath done all His share toward it), every wicked man takes his head from the blessing, and rather chooses that the devils should rejoice in his destruction, than that his Lord should triumph in his felicity. And now upon the supposition of these premises, we may imagine that it will be an infinite amazement to meet that Lord to be our Judge whose person we have murdered, whose honor we have disparaged, whose purposes we have destroyed, whose joys we have lessened, whose passion we have made ineffectual, and whose love we have trampled under our profane and impious feet.

But there is yet a third part of this consideration. As it will be inquired at the day of judgment concerning the dishonors to the person of Christ, so also concerning the profession and institution of Christ, and concerning His poor members; for by these also we make sad reflections upon our Lord. Every man that lives wickedly disgraces the religion and institution of Jesus, he discourages strangers from entering into it, he weakens the hands of them that are in already, and makes that the adversaries speak reproachfully of the name of Christ; but although it is certain our Lord and Judge will deeply resent all these things, yet there is one thing which He takes more tenderly, and that is, the uncharitableness of men toward His poor. It shall then be upbraided to them by the Judge, that Himself was hungry and they refused to give meat to Him; that gave them His body and heart-blood to feed them and quench their thirst; that they denied a robe to cover His nakedness, and yet He would have clothed their souls with the robe of His righteousness, lest their souls should be found naked on the day of the Lord's visitation; and all this unkindness is nothing but that evil men were uncharitable to their brethren, they would not feed the hungry, nor give drink to the thirsty nor clothe the naked, nor relieve their brothers' needs, nor forgive their follies, nor cover their shame, nor turn their eyes from delighting in their affronts and evil accidents; this is it which our Lord will take so tenderly, that His brethren for whom He died, who sucked the paps of His mother, that fed on His body and are nourished with His blood, whom He hath lodged in His heart and entertains in His bosom, the partners of His spirit and co-heirs of His inheritance, that these should be denied relief and suffered to go away ashamed, and unpitied; this our blessed Lord will take so ill, that all those who are guilty of this unkindness, have no reason to expect the favor of the Court.

## The Might of the Judge

To this if we add the almightiness of the Judge, His infinite wisdom and knowledge of all causes, and all persons, and all circumstances, that He is infinitely just, inflexibly angry, and impartial in His sentence, there can be nothing added either to the greatness or the requisites of a terrible and an almighty Judge. For who can resist Him who is almighty? Who can evade His scrutiny that knows all things? Who can hope for pity of Him that is inflexible? Who can think to be exempted when the Judge is righteous and impartial? But in all these annexes of the Great Judge, that which I shall now remark, is that indeed which hath terror in it, and that is, the severity of our Lord. For then is the day of vengeance and recompenses, and no mercy at all shall be showed, but to them that are the sons of mercy; for the other, their portion is such as can be expected from these premises.

If we remember the instances of God's severity in this life, in the days of mercy and repentance, in those days when judgment waits upon mercy, and received laws by the rules and measures of pardon, and that for all the rare streams of loving kindness issuing out of paradise and refreshing all our fields with a moisture more fruitful than the floods of Nilus, still there are mingled some storms and violences, some fearful instances of the divine justice, we may more readily expect it will be worse, infinitely worse, at that day, when judgment shall ride in triumph, and mercy shall be the accuser of the wicked. But so we read, and are commanded to remember, because they are written for our example, that God destroyed at once five cities of the plain, and all the country, and Sodom and her sisters are set forth for an example, suffering vengeance of eternal fire.

Fearful it was when God destroyed at once twenty-three thousand for fornication, and an exterminating angel in one night killed one hundred and eighty-five thousand of the Assyrian, and the first-born of all the families of Egypt, and for the sin of David in numbering the people, three score and ten thousand of the people, died, and God sent ten tribes into captivity and eternal oblivion and indistinction from a common people for their idolatry. Did not God strike Korah and his company with fire from heaven? and the earth opened and swallowed up the congregation of Abiram? And is not evil come upon all the world for one sin of Adam? Did not the anger of God break the nation of the Jews all in pieces with judgments so great, that no nation ever suffered the like, because none ever sinned so? And at once it was done, that God in anger destroyed all the world, and eight persons only escaped the angry baptism of water, and yet this world is the time of mercy; God hath opened here His magazines, and sent His Holy Son as the great channel and fountain of it, too: here He delights in mercy, and in judgment loved to remember it, and it triumphs over all His works, and God contrives instruments and accidents, chances and designs, occasions and opportunities for mercy. If, therefore, now the anger of God makes such terrible eruptions upon the wicked people that delight in sin, how great may we suppose that anger to be, how severe that judgment, how terrible that vengeance, how intolerable those inflictions which God reserves for the full effusion of indignation on the great day of vengeance!

We may also guess at it by this: if God upon all single instances, and in the midst of our sins, before they are come to the full, and sometimes in the beginning of an evil habit, be so fierce in His anger, what can we imagine it to be in that day when the wicked are to drink the dregs of that horrid potion, and count over all the particulars of their whole treasure of wrath? "This is the day of wrath, and God shall reveal, or bring forth, His righteous judgments." The expression is taken from Deuteronomy 32:34: "Is not this laid up in store with me, and sealed up among my treasures? I will restore it in the day of vengeance, for the Lord shall judge His people, and repent Himself for His servants." For so did the Lybian lion that was brought up under discipline, and taught to endure blows, and eat the meat of order and regular provision, and to suffer gentle usages and the familiarities of societies; but once he brake out into his own wildness, and killed two Roman boys; but those forage in the Lybian mountains tread down and devour all that they meet or master; and when they have fasted two days, lay up an anger great as is their appetite, and bring certain death to all that can be overcome.

God is pleased to compare Himself to a lion; and though in this life He hath confined Himself with promises and gracious emanations of an infinite goodness, and limits Himself by conditions and covenants, and suffers Himself to be overcome by prayers, and Himself hath invented ways of atonement and expiation; yet when He is provoked by our unhandsome and unworthy actions, He makes sudden breaches, and tears some of us in pieces, and of others He breaks their bones or affrights their hopes and secular gaieties, and fills their house with mourning and cypress, and groans and death. But when this Lion of the tribe of Judah shall appear upon His own mountain, the mountain and that justice shall have her chain and golden fetters taken off, then justice shall strike, and mercy shall hold her hands; she shall strike sore strokes, and pity shall not break the blow; and God shall account with us by minutes, and for words, and for thoughts, and then He shall be severe to mark what is done amiss; and that justice may reign entirely, God shall open the wicked man's treasure, and tell the sums, and weigh grains and scruples. Said Philo upon the place of Deuteronomy before quoted: As there are treasures of good thing, and God has crowns and scepters in store for His saints and servants, and coronets and martyrs, and rosaries for virgins, and vials full of prayers, and bottle full of tears, and a register of sighs and penitential groans, so God hath a treasure of wrath and fury, of scourges and scorpions, and then shall be produced the shame of lust, and the malice of envy, and the groans of the oppressed, and the persecutions of the saints, and the cares of covetousness, and the troubles of ambition, and the insolences of traitors, and the violence of rebels, and the rage of anger, and the uneasiness of impatience, and the restlessness of unlawful desires; and by this time the monsters and diseases will be numerous and intolerable, when God's heavy hand shall press the *sanies* and the intolerableness, the obliquity and the unreasonableness, the amazement and the disorder, the smart and the sorrow, the guilt and the punishment, out from all our sins, and pour them into one chalice, and mingle them with an infinite wrath, and make the wicked drink of all the vengeance, and force it down their unwilling throats with the violence of devils and accursed spirits.

## The Severity of the Judge

We may guess at the severity of the Judge by the lesser strokes of that judgment which He is pleased to send upon sinners in this world, to make them afraid of the horrible pains of doomsday—I mean the torments of an unquiet conscience, the amazement and confusions of some sins and some persons. For I have sometimes seen persons surprised in a base action, and taken in the circumstances of crafty theft and secret injustices, before their excuse was ready. They have changed their color, their speech hath faltered, their tongue stammered, their eyes did wander and fix nowhere, till shame made them sink into their hollow eye-pits to retreat from the images and circumstances of discovery; their wits are lost, their reason useless, the whole order of their soul is decomposed, and they neither see, nor feel, nor think, as they used to do, but they are broken into disorder by a stroke of damnation and a lesser stripe of hell; but then if you come to observe a guilty and a base murderer, a condemned traitor, and see him harassed first by an evil conscience, and then pulled in pieces by the hangman's hooks, or broken upon sorrows and the wheel, we may then guess (as well as we can in this life) what the pains of that day shall be to accursed souls. But those we shall consider afterward in their proper scene; now only we are to estimate the severity of our Judge by the intolerableness of an evil conscience; if guilt will make a man despair—and despair will make a man mad, confounded, and dissolved in all the regions of his senses and more noble faculties, that he shall neither feel, nor hear, nor see anything but specters and illusions, devils and frightful dreams, and hear noises, and shriek fearfully, and look pale and distracted, like a hopeless man from the horrors and confusions of a lost battle, upon which all his hopes did stand—then the wicked must at the day of judgment expect strange things and fearful, and such which now no language can express, and then no patience can endure. Then only it can truly be said that he is inflexible and inexorable. No prayers then can move Him, no groans can cause Him to pity thee; therefore pity thyself in time, that when the Judge comes thou mayest be one of the sons of everlasting mercy, to whom pity belongs as part of thine inheritance, for all else shall without any remorse (except His own) be condemned by the horrible sentence.

That all may think themselves concerned in this consideration, let us remember that even the righteous and most innocent shall pass through a severe trial. Many of the ancients explicated this severity by the fire of conflagration, which say they shall purify those souls at the day of judgment, which in this life have built upon the foundation (hay and stubble) works of folly and false opinions, states of imperfection. So St. Augustine's doctrine was: "The great fire at doomsday shall throw some into the portion of the left hand, and others shall be purified and represented on the right." And the same is affirmed by Origen and Lactantius; and St. Hilary thus expostulates: "Since we are to give account for every idle word, shall we long for the day of judgment, wherein we must, everyone of us, pass that unwearied fire in which those grievous punishments for expiating the soul from sins must be endured; for to such as have been baptized with the Holy Spirit it remaineth that they be consummated with the fire of judgment." And St. Ambrose adds: "That if any be as Peter or as John, they are baptized with this fire, and he that is purged here had need to be purged there again. Let him also purify us, that everyone of us being burned with that flaming sword, not burned up or consumed, we may enter into Paradise, and give thanks unto the Lord who hath brought us into a place of refreshment." This opinion of theirs is, in the main of it, very uncertain; relying upon the sense of some obscure place of Scripture is only apt to represent the great severity of the Judge at that day, and it hath in it this only certainty, that even the most innocent person hath great need of mercy, and he that hath the greatest cause of confidence, although he runs to no rocks to hide him, yet he runs to the protection of the cross, and hides himself under the shadow of the divine mercies: and he that shall receive the absolution of the blessed sentence shall also suffer the terrors of the day, and the fearful circumstances of Christ's coming. The effect of this consideration is this: That if the righteous scarcely be saved, where shall the wicked and the sinner appear? And if St. Paul, whose conscience accused him not, yet durst not be too confident, because he was not hereby justified, but might be found faulty by the severer judgment of his Lord, how shall we appear, with all our crimes and evil habits round about us? If there be need of much mercy to the servants and friends of the Judge, then His enemies shall not be able to stand upright in judgment.

## The Sentence of the Judge

Let us consider the circumstances of our appearing and His sentence; and first I consider that men at the day of judgment that belong not to the portion of life, shall have three sorts of accusers: 1. Christ Himself, who is their judge; 2. Their own conscience, whom they have injured and blotted with characters of death and foul dishonor; 3. The devil, their enemy, whom they served.

Christ shall be their accuser, not only upon the stock of those direct injuries (which I before reckoned) of crucifying the Lord of Life, once and again, etc., but upon the titles of contempt and unworthiness, of unkindness and ingratitude; and the accusation will be nothing else but a plain representation of those artifices and assistances, those bonds and invitations, those constrainings and importunities, which our dear Lord used to us to make it almost impossible to lie in sin, and necessary to be saved. For it will, it must needs be, a fearful exprobration of our unworthiness, when the Judge Himself shall bear witness against us that the wisdom of God Himself was strangely employed in bringing us safely to felicity. I shall draw a short scheme which, although it must needs be infinitely short, of what God hath done for us, yet it will be enough to shame us. God did not only give His Son for an example, and the Son gave Himself for a price for us, but both gave the Holy Spirit to assist us in mighty graces, for the verifications of faith, and the entertainments of hope, and the increase and perseverance of charity. God gave to us a new nature, He put another principle into us, a third part of a perfective constitution; we have the spirit put into us, to be a part of us, as properly to produce actions of a holy life, as the soul of man in the body does produce the natural. God hath exalted human nature, and made it in the person of Jesus Christ, to sit above the highest seat of angels, and the angels are made ministering spirits, ever since their Lord became our brother. Christ hath by a miraculous sacrament given us His body to eat and His blood to drink; He made ways that we may become all one with Him. He hath given us an easy religion, and hath established our future felicity upon natural and pleasant conditions, and we are to be happy hereafter if we suffer God to make us happy here; and things are so ordered that a man must take more pains to perish than to be happy. God hath found out rare ways to make our prayers acceptable, our weak petitions, the desires of our imperfect souls, to prevail mightily with God, and to lay a holy violence and an undeniable necessity upon Himself; and God will deny us nothing but when we ask of Him to do us ill offices, to give us poisons and dangers, and evil nourishment, and temptations; and He that hath given such mighty power to the prayers of His servants, yet will not be moved by those potent and mighty prayers to do any good man an evil turn, or to grant him one mischief—in that only God can deny us. But in all things else God hath made all the excellent things in heaven and earth to join toward the holy and fortunate effects; for He that appointed an angel to present the prayers of saints, and Christ makes intercession for us, and the Holy Spirit makes intercession for us with us groans unutterable, and all the holy men in the world pray for all and for everyone, and God hath instructed us with Scriptures, and precedents, and collateral and direct assistances to pray, and He encouraged us with divers excellent promises, and parables, and examples, and teaches us what to pray, and how, and gives one promise to public prayer, and another to private prayer, and to both the blessing of being heard.

Add to this account that God did heap blessings upon us without order, infinitely, perpetually, and in all instances, when we needed and when we needed not. He heard us when we prayed, giving us all, and giving us more, than we desired. He desired that we should ask, and yet He hath also prevented our desires. He watched for us, and at His own charge sent a whole order of men whose employment is to minister to our souls; and if all this had not been enough, He had given us more also. He promised heaven to our obedience, a province for a dish of water, a kingdom for a prayer, satisfaction for desiring it, grace for receiving, and more grace for accepting and using the first. He invited us with gracious words and perfect entertainments; He threatened horrible things to us if we would not be happy; He hath made strange necessities for us, making our very repentance to be a conjugation of holy actions, and holy times, and a long succession; He hath taken away all excuses from us; He hath called us from temptation; He bears our charges, He is always beforehand with us in every act of favor, and perpetually slow in striking, and His arrows are unfeathered; and He is so long, first, in drawing His sword, and another long while in whetting it, and yet longer in lifting His hand to strike, that before the blow comes the man hath repented long, unless he be a fool and impudent; and then God is so glad of an excuse to lay His anger aside, that certainly, if after all this, we refuse life and glory, there is no more to be said; this plain story will condemn us; but the story is very much longer; and, as our conscience will represent all our sins to us, so the Judge will represent all His Father's kindnesses, as Nathan did to David, when he was to make the justice of the divine sentence appear against him. Then it shall be remembered that the joys of every day's piety would have been a greater pleasure every night than the remembrance of every night's sin could have been in the morning; that every night the trouble and labor of the day's virtue would have been as much passed and turned to as the pleasure of that day's sin, but that they would be infinitely distinguished by the effects. The offering ourselves to God every morning, and the thanksgiving to God every night, hope and fear, shame and desire, the honor of leaving a fair name behind us, and the shame of dying like a fool—everything indeed in the world is made to be an argument and an inducement to us to invite us to come to God and be saved; and therefore when this, and infinitely more shall by the Judge be exhibited in sad remembrances, there needs no other sentence; we shall condemn ourselves with a hasty shame and a fearful confusion, to see how good God hath been to us, and how base we have been to ourselves. Thus Moses is said to accuse the Jews; and thus also He that does accuse, is said to condemn, as Verres was by Cicero, and Claudia by Domitius her accuser, and the world of impenitent persons by the men of Nineveh, and all by Christ, their Judge. I represent the horror of this circumstance to consist in this, besides the reasonableness of the judgment, and the certainty of the condemnation, it cannot but be an argument of an intolerable despair to perishing souls, when He that was our advocate all our life, shall, in the day of that appearing, be our Accuser and our Judge, a party against us, an injured person in the day of His power and of His wrath, doing execution upon all His own foolish and malicious enemies.

Our conscience shall be our accuser. But this signifies but these two things: First, that we shall be condemned for the evils that we have done and shall then remember, God by His power wiping away the dust from the tables or our memory, and taking off the consideration and the voluntary neglect and rude shufflings of our cases of conscience. For then we shall see things as they are, the evil circumstances and the crooked intentions, the adherent unhandsomeness and the direct crimes; for all things are laid up safely, and though we draw a curtain of cobweb over them, and a few fig-leaves before our shame, yet God shall draw away the curtain, and forgetfulness shall be no more, because, with a taper in the hand of God, all the corners of our nastiness shall be discovered. And, secondly, it signifies this also, that not only the justice of God shall be confessed by us in our own shame and condemnation, but the evil of the sentence shall be received into us, to melt our bowels and to break our heart in pieces within us, because we are the authors of our own death, and our own inhuman hands have torn our souls in pieces. Thus far the horrors are great, and when evil men consider it, it is certain they must be afraid to die. Even they that have lived well, have some sad considerations, and the tremblings of humility, and suspicion of themselves. I remember St. Cyprian tells of a good man who in his agony of death saw a fantasm of a noble and angelical shape, who, frowning and angry, said to him: "Ye cannot endure sickness, ye are troubled at the evils of the world, and yet you are loath to die and to be quit of them; what shall I do to you?" Although this is apt to represent every man's condition more or less, yet, concerning persons of wicked lives, it hath in it too many sad degrees of truth; they are impatient of sorrow, and justly fearful of death, because they know not how to comfort themselves in the evil accidents of their lives; and their conscience is too polluted to take death for sanctuary, and to hope to have amends made to their condition by the sentence of the day of judgment. Evil and sad is their condition who cannot be contented here nor blessed hereafter whose life is their misery and their conscience is their enemy, whose grave is their prison and death their undoing, and the sentence of doomsday the beginning of an intolerable condition.

### The Description of the Devils

The third sort of accusers are the devils, and they will do it with malicious and evil purposes. The prince of the devils hath Diabolus for one of his chiefest appellatives. The accuser of the brethren he is by his professed malice and employment; and therefore God, who delights that His mercy should triumph and His goodness prevail over all the malice of men and devils, hath appointed one whose office is to reprove the accuser and to resist the enemy, and to be a defender of their cause who belong to God. The Holy Spirit is a defender; the evil spirit is the accuser; and they that in this life belong to one or the other, shall in the same proportion be treated at the day of judgment. The devil shall accuse the brethren, that is, the saints and servants of God, and shall tell concerning their follies and infirmities, the sins of their youth and weakness of their age, the imperfect grace and the long schedule of omissions of duty, their scruples and their fears, their diffidences and pusillanimity, and all those things which themselves by strict examination find themselves guilty of and have confessed all their shame and the matter of their sorrows, their evil intentions and their little plots, their carnal confidences and too fond adherences of the things of this world, their indulgence and easiness of government, their wilder joys and freer meals, their loss of time and their too forward and apt compliances, their trifling arrests and little peevishnesses, the mixtures of the world with the thing of the Spirit, and all the incidences of humanity he will bring forth and aggravate them by circumstances of ingratitude, and the breach of promise, and the evacuating all their holy purposes, and breaking their resolutions, and rifling their vows, and all these things, being drawn into an entire representment, and the bills clogged by numbers, will make the best man in the world seem foul and unhandsome, and stained with the characters of death and evil dishonor.

But for these there is appointed a defender. The Holy Spirit that maketh intercession for us shall then also interpose, and against all these things shall oppose the passion of our blessed Lord, and upon all their defects shall cast the robe of righteousness; and the sins of their youth shall not prevail so much as the repentance of their age, and their omissions be excused by probable intervening causes, and their little escapes shall appear single and in disunion, because they were always kept asunder by penitential prayers and sighings, and their seldom returns of sin by their daily watchfulness, and their often infirmities by the sincerity of their souls, and their scruples by their zeal, and their passions by their love, and all by the mercies of God and the sacrifice which their Judge offered and the Holy Spirit made effective by daily graces and assistances. These, therefore, infallibly go to the portion of the right hand, because the Lord our God shall answer for them. But as for the wicked, it is not so with them; for although the plain story of their life be to them a sad condemnation, yet what will be answered when it shall be told concerning them, that they despised God's mercies, and feared not His angry judgments; that they regarded not His Word, and loved not His excellences; that they were not persuaded by the promises nor affrighted by His threatenings; that they neither would accept His government nor His blessings; that all the sad stories that ever happened in both the world (in all which Himself did escape till the day of His death, and was not concerned in them save only that He was called upon by everyone of them, which He ever heard or saw or as told of, to repentance), that all these were sent to Him in vain?

But cannot the accuser truly say to the Judge concerning such persons, "They were Thine by creation, but mine by their own choice; Thou didst redeem them indeed, but they sold themselves to me for a trifle, or for an unsatisfying interest; Thou diedst for them, but they obeyed my commandments; I gave them nothing, I promised them nothing but the filthy pleasures of a night, or the joys of madness, or the delights of a disease; I never hanged upon the cross three long hours for them, nor endured the labors of a poor life thirty-three years together for their interest; only when they were Thine by the merit of Thy death, they quickly became mine by the demerit of their ingratitude; and when Thou hadst clothed their soul with Thy robe, and adorned them by Thy graces, and only put on a robe of darkness, and they thought themselves secure and went dancing to their grave like a drunkard to a fight, or a fly unto a candle; and therefore they that did partake with us in our faults must divide with us in our portion and fearful interest."

This is a sad story because it ends in death and there is nothing to abate or lessen the calamity. It concerns us therefore to consider in time that he that tempts us will accuse us, and what he calls pleasant now he shall then say was nothing, and all the gains that now invite earthly souls and mean persons to vanity, was nothing but the seeds of folly, and the harvest in pain and sorrow and shame eternal. But then, since this horror proceeds upon the account of so many accusers, God hath put it in our power by a timely accusation of ourselves in the tribunal of the court Christian, to prevent all the arts of aggravation which at doomsday shall load foolish and undiscerning souls. He that accuses himself of his crimes here, means to forsake them, and looks upon them on all sides, and spies out his deformity, and is taught to hate them, he is instructed and prayed for, he prevents the anger of God and defeats the devil's malice, and, by making shame the instrument of repentance, he takes away the sin, and makes that to be his medicine which otherwise would be his death: and, concerning this exercise, I shall only add what the patriarch of Alexandria told an old religious person in his hermitage. Having asked him what he found in that desert, he was answered, "Only this, to judge and condemn myself perpetually; that is the employment of my solitude." The patriarch answered, "There is no other way." By accusing ourselves we shall make the devil's malice useless, and our own consciences clear, and be reconciled to the Judge by the severities of an early repentance, and then we need to fear no accusers.

## Work and Watching

**John Ker** (1819-1886) is little known today, but in his day he was a respected preacher and professor of preaching and pastoral work at the United Free Church Seminary in Glasgow, Scotland.

He published two volumes of sermons: this one is from the *Sermons First Series*, published in Edinburgh in 1870 by Edmonston and Douglas.

John Ker

# 9

# WORK AND WATCHING

> The Son of Man is as a man taking a far journey, who left his house, and . . . gave to every man his work, and commanded the porter to watch (Mark 13:34).

THE CHRISTIAN CHURCH is here compared to a great house or palace left for a time by its Lord and Master, the Son of Man. He left His church at His ascension, and He will return again to take account of it at the general judgment in the end of the world. He comes at the same time to every individual at his death. The Son of Man at His departure gave authority to His servant, that is, not merely, as some say, to the office-bearers of His church, but to all His servants, authority to transact in His room, to maintain due order in the house, and seek its good. There is meanwhile no other above them in the house, no earthly master, but only the Word of Christ, which under the teaching of His Spirit He has left for their guidance. Besides this authority to maintain order in the house, it is said, "He gave to every man his work, and commanded the porter to watch." This is the most important portion of Christ's parting charge, since the rule and order of the house are there only for the sake of the work and watching in it. It is to these that we shall now turn attention, taking, *first*, the work of the servants; *second*, the watch of the porter; and *third*, the bearing of each of these upon the other.

## The Work of the Servants

I. And here we observe that *work is the common duty of all in Christ's house*. It would be very strange if were not so. The first thing we read of God doing for man, when He made him, was to assign him work. Before He gave him a right to eat of the fruit of the trees, "He put him into the garden of Eden to dress it and to keep it" (Gen. 2:15). When man is translated to the heavenly Eden it is not to idleness—"they serve him day and night in his temple." The wise man when he looked abroad on the world made this deep reflection—"all things are full of labor." The calm stars are in ceaseless motion, and every leaf is a world, with its busy inhabitants, and the sap coursing through its veins as the life-blood through our own. He who made all worlds has said, "My Father worketh hitherto, and I work." It would be strange then if the Christian church, which was intended to be the beating heart to all the world's activities, were exempted from a law so universal. It was for this end that Christ called its members into it—"why stand ye here all the day idle?" and then "gave to every man his work." Were it otherwise, it would be against our best and highest nature. Work is not only a duty but a blessing. Every right deed is a step in the upward scale of being by which we are raised to that rich reward—"Well done, good and faithful servant, enter thou into the joy of thy Lord." That joy is itself larger and nobler employment near the throne of Him who has risen to heaven, not for idle repose, but grander action. If any one is ready to complain of the urgent voices that summon him to labor, of Christ's command, "Son, go work today in my vineyard," of the pressing wants of the household that seem to grow in piercing earnestness, of fellow-servants who plead for aid, and fellow-sinners whose miseries cry for pity, let such an one remember that this is the ordinance of a Wise Master who set us the example of unwearied labor, finishing one work to begin another—that it is the law of the universe of that God who fainteth not neither is weary in deeds of kindness to His creatures—and that it is in this way God and His Christ lift us up to the blessed dignity of being their fellow-workers. Instead of praying that God would grant us less work, our request should be that He would give us a greater heart and growing strength to meet all its claims.

We observe next that this work of Christ's house *is varied to different individuals*. "The Son of Man gave to every one, that is, to each one, his work." In one respect there is something common in the work of all, as there is a common salvation. "This is the work of God, that ye believe in Him who He hath sent"—"This is the will of God, even your sanctification." We have said this is common work for each one, and yet even here there may be a variety in the form. There is a different color of beauty in different stones that are all of them precious. One man may be burnishing to the sparkle of the diamond, while another is depending to the glow of the ruby. For this reason there are such different temperaments in Christian character, and varying circumstances in Christian life, that the foundation of the wall of the city may be garnished with all manner of precious stones. Each Christian has his own place and luster in that temple, and therefore there is no ground to disparage our neighbor, and none to despair of ourselves, if we are both in the hand of Christ. When we look from the individual life to the practical work, the variety is still more marked. There are different members, and all have not the same office. Some are there to teach—some to counsel and administer—some to tend the young—some to visit the sickbed—some to conduct the temporal affairs of the church—some to be liberal givers as God has prospered them, and some, without any formal mode of action, come under this description, which applies to them all, "sons of God, without rebuke, shining as lights in the world, holding forth the Word of Life." It is very beautiful to see how the God, who has bound His world into a grand harmony by its very diversity, has arranged for this same end in His church, by giving the members their different faculties of work—how the pure light that touches the palace-house of Christ with its varied cornices and turrets till every color lies in tranquil beauty beside its fellow. If it is not so it should be so, and as the church grows it will be so. Use and ornament, the cornerstone and the copestone, shall both be felt to have their due place. To see how this may be, is to perceive that an end can be put to all jealousies and heart-burnings, and may help us even now to take our position calmly and unenviously, working in our department, assured that our labor will be found to contribute to the full proportion of the whole.

Another remark is that *each individual has means for ascertaining his own work.* The Son of Man "*gave* to every man his work." The Master of the house let each servant know what he was expected to attend to, and it must be supposed that Christ will have some means by which He gives a man intimation of what He looks for from him. It is very vain to seek this as some have done, in any personal revelation, or any irresistible impression made on the mind. Christ guides men into their sphere of work by the finger of His providence, and by the enlightenment of His Word in the hand of His Spirit. A man is to try to find his place of usefulness in the church of Christ very much as he tries to find it in the world of men, and indeed these two generally go together. If it be sometimes difficult to ascertain this, it may be well to remember that this very difficulty is part of our training. It might be a much simpler and a more satisfactory thing meanwhile to have our place directly pointed out to us, but it would not make us so strong in the end.

It is of importance to have some rules to guide us in choosing Christian work, and the first we mention is to consider *for what we are most fitted.* There is scarcely anyone who has not some specialty, both as a man and a Christian, which makes him suited for some particular service, and it should be his aim to discover this. There is of course the danger of judging too favorably of ourselves, and running where we are not called, and the opposite danger of our diffidence or inertness that leads some to hide their talent in the earth; but in general, if a man will be true and honest, he may with God's help come to know what his power for usefulness is. An important guide in this respect is the opinion of our fellow-men when fairly expressed. If there be a strong appeal from them for our help in a good work, it should do much to counterbalance a sense of our own unfitness. This is one of the marked ways in which Christ speaks to us.

Another rule is to consider well *where God has placed us*—our position in life, our opportunities for particular action or influence, the paths in which we move in society, the leisure that lies in our hand. To examine these carefully, and see how we can with all wisdom turn them to Christian profit, is a great matter for every one of us. If there be an earnest desire to do good even with a sense of much unfitness, it is marvelous how fitness will grow. He who sends the opportunity and the desire will send the qualification, and I do not know of any nobler encomium from the lips of the Great Master than this, "She hath done what she could." The thought of having it from Him at last may strengthen our weak hands and make our hearts leap for joy. In general, I believe it will be found that the best Christian work is not far from our own door, and that those are mistaken who think they can do nothing till they find some great sphere, and who run hither and thither in search of it. Church agencies have their high value, in some respects they are indispensable, but it would be sad indeed if they could measure in their records all the work of Christ's servants. It is often most effectually performed when it is done in no church connection, but noiselessly and informally, in hidden nooks of quiet homes, or walking by the wayside and yet scattering seed in the field. A master among his servants, a workman among his associates, a mother among her children, a sister among brothers, may be dropping words and radiating influences of which there shall be no report till the last great disclosure shall bring out the "Well done, good and faithful servant." The greatest work of the Christian church should be this natural outgoing of its own life—a life which should obliterate the distinction between the religious and the secular, and make them both one—all work, religion—and all life, worship. Here there is room for each one, whether in the busy world or the calmest retreat; and if we only carefully seek to know *what* we are and *where* we are, and put the question prayerfully, "Lord, what wilt thou have me to do?" we shall find that the Son of Man has given us our work, and that He will give us also strength and fitness for it.

### The Watch of the Porter

II. We come now to consider, in the *second* place, the watch of the porter—"and commanded the porter to watch."

The porter is that one of the servants whose station is at the door to look out for those who approach, and open to them if they have right to enter. Are we to understand that the body of the servants are exempted from watching while one takes the duty for them? This would be against the bearing of the whole Bible and of Christ's own teaching. In verse 37 of this chapter, He guards us against such a misapprehension, "What I say unto you, I say unto all, Watch." The object of our Lord is, by telling us that the workmen are many and the watchman one, to impress this lesson, that, while the mode of labor in the house may vary, there is something common to all who are in it—the duty of watchfulness. The porter must stand at the door of every heart while that heart pursues its work.

What are we to understand then by the watch of the porter? Some say it is prayer—to be constantly fulfilling that injunction, "Pray without ceasing." And certainly prayer is closely connected with watching. The two are frequently conjoined by Christ, "Watch and pray." "Watch unto prayer." But this combination of them shows that they differ, for Scripture uses no vain repetitions. The parable itself will disclose the meaning. The master of the house is absent and the period of His return is uncertain. The porter is stationed at the door to look out for the signs of His coming, and give timely notice of it. He is to have his eye turned also inward upon the arrangements of the house, that they may be in readiness for the Lord's return. This return of Christ is at the end of the world, to take account not only of His professed servants, but of all men, and there can be no doubt that from the moment of His departure He has charged His church to expect His re-appearance, and to perform all her service in view of it. When the cloud received Him, and His disciples looked up to it as to a door that closed on a departing friend, the angelic attendants assured them, "This same Jesus shall so come as ye have seen Him go into heaven," and when we gaze up into that broad sky in the glory of day or mystery of night, we should strive to realize the time when it shall part again and restore our unseen Lord.

The Book of Revelation which concludes the canon of the Word shows the attitude of the church—her eye searching the future, her arms outstretched in longing as His were in blessing, and the sigh breathing from her heart, "Even so, come, Lord Jesus."

This great event is constantly represented in the New Testament as near, and the view is natural and true. Never does the meeting with a beloved friend come so close to us as when we have just parted from him. Love makes the tears of farewells sparkle into welcomes; and if we could only retain the same impression of Christ's loss, His return would be as nigh. It is moreover, in the New Testament, the great event that towers above every other. The heaven, that gives back Christ, gives back all we have loved and lost, solves all doubts, and ends all sorrows. His coming looks in upon the whole life of His church, as a lofty mountain peak looks in upon every little valley and sequestered home around its base, and belongs to them all alike. Every generation lies under the shadow of it, for whatever is transcendently great is constantly near, and in moments of high conviction it absorbs petty interests and annihilates intervals. It may surely be for us to consider, whether our removal of Christ's coming further from us in feeling does not arise from a less vivid impression of its reality and surpassing moment. Such views depend in no way upon peculiar opinions regarding His advent, for the longing expectancy of His appearance should be as common to all Christians as is their hope, and a thousand years are as a day to the grand event which opens everlasting life. What is the crust of a few centuries or millenniums, if the great ocean of eternity be felt heaving underneath, surging up through the chasms which death reveals, and admonishing through us of the time when it shall sweep away all barriers and leave nothing but is own infinite bosom?

To be constantly realizing this, and living and laboring in the prospect of it, is, we believe, what is here enjoined in the admonition "to watch." It is to do all our work with the thought of His eye measuring it, as of a friend who is ever present to our soul, gone from us in outward form, sure to return, and meanwhile near in spirit—to subject our plans and acts to His approval, asking ourselves at every step how this would please Him, shrinking from what would cloud His face, rejoicing with great joy in all that would meet His smile. If God has taken from us earthly friends, and if we continue to think of them with the warm love of earth mingling in the awe of the unseen, it is to help us to rise to the conception of that greatest Friend who will bring them back at His return and give us their approval in His own. At the same time there is included, in the view of Christ's coming, the thought of our own death, which brings each one of us close up to His second advent, whensoever it may be. Every life has an end, as momentous to it as the end of the world, for it places it immediately before the judgment-seat, and subjects it to the omniscient eye. The peculiarity of the Christian view is that our own death and Christ's coming are seen in one line of perspective, and that all our work should be done looking for that blessed hope, "the glorious appearing of the great God, our Savior Jesus Christ."

It is in most cases a much harder thing to preserve this watchful heart than to have our hands busy with the work of the house, and therefore, probably, the emphasis which our Lord puts on it—"He *gave* to every man his work"—"He *commanded* the porter to watch." But, if attended to, it will bring its proportionate benefit. It will keep all wakeful, for nothing is so fitted to rouse from the lethargy that falls on every spirit as the thought of the day of His coming. It will preserve purity if we have before us those eyes that are like a flame of fire, and so we shall "give all diligence to be found of Him without spot, and blameless." It will maintain the soul in calmness, for not those who are heedless feel the depth of security, but those who have set their watch and go their steadfast rounds. And it will rise increasingly to the fervor of prayer—that prayer which is the strength of the soul and the life of all work. The thought of that grand presence, which shall break down through the skies to fill our world, and test and renew all things, will make our hearts burn up like a fire to meet Him—"Watch ye therefore, and pray always, that ye may be accounted worthy to escape all these things that shall come to pass, and to stand before the Son of Man" (Luke 21:36).

## The Bearing of These Two Duties upon Each Other

III. We come now, in the *third* place, to show the bearing of these two duties upon each other.

On the one hand, work cannot be rightly performed without watching. If watching were absent, work would be *blind, and without a purpose*. It would be work without a proper crowning close, and without a master to sum up all its results. The foresight of the conclusion to which we are advancing makes us intelligent fellow-laborers with God, and helps us to concentrate our efforts on the one great issue. It is this which lifts Christianity above all the philosophies. They can only wish or guess what the future may bring, and can work vaguely in the house, but have no watchman at the door. They may have the hand and the foot, but they want the eye and the ear which can perceive already the signs and opening harmonies of a new world—which learn from the mind of Christ the preparations that are needed for the kingdom which is righteousness and peace and joy.

If watching were absent, work would become *discouraging and tedious*. It would stretch away endlessly into a limitless future, where each man's effort would disappear in the general mass of human struggle, like rivers in a shadowy, shoreless sea. We could not long have heart for such work where we could neither perceive one grand consummation nor the share we were to have in helping it. But now the coming of Christ tells us there is a fixed and most blissful close, and every earnest man, and every earnest effort, will be found to have a part in hastening it. There is no selfishness in being stimulated by this, for it is a divine desire to be made like God, channels of life and happiness, and it is but a portion of the heart of Him who renounced self, and who, for such a joy, endured the cross and despised the shame. If we would see its results we have only to compare the fitful efforts of any human system with the eighteen hundred years from the thought of a departed and returning Christ.

If watching were absent, work would become *formal and dead*. The labor of the hands, as we all feel, degenerates quickly into barren routine, if there be not a constant effort to keep the heart fresh. Duty can never live long separate from truth, Christian service from Christ. There must be oil in the lamp if it is to burn. It is watching unto prayer that brings in this Divine life, that quickens the powers, and makes them rise up for new and higher work. The special danger of our age is that we may lose perception of the real soul and end of all our labor in the multiplied machinery that carries it on. Our very Christian activities will lead to decline and death if spiritual life is not growing within, in proportion to them—if we are not realizing more strongly our own individual spiritual wants, living more in the presence of eternity, and remembering that admonition which stands connected with Christ—"Be watchful, and strengthen the things which remain, that are ready to die."

But if work cannot be performed without watching, on the other hand, watching will not suffice without work.

Without work, watching would be *solitary*. There do seem times when God shuts a heart up to this—when pining sickness or sore bereavement makes work impossible or utterly distasteful, and one feels as if he could only hold himself above despair, and look out for that Christ who is to heal all. And yet we believe there is no one in this world irretrievably condemned to such a life. The loneliest sickbed, the darkest chamber of sorrow, never loses the power of Christian influence, and He who trod the winepress alone, and all the while was saving others—who made His cross a place to preach comfort from—surely teaches us how possible it is, and how noble, for a crushed and broken heart to forget itself. Then it is doing its greatest work for Christ, and drawing to it the hand that will find its cruel wounds and give it all its desire. We may make the night solitary of all service, and bury our soul in bitter musings; but we should rather thank God that there is no spot on earth where some duty does not still remain, and, in the calm steadfast pursuance of it, we should beguile the hours of the night till "the day break and the shadows flee away."

Without work, watching is *subject to many temptations*: There are men who have placed the essence of the Christian life in solitude and contemplation, and imagined they were thereby fleeing from the world's dangers and their own passions. It is against the example of Christ and all His apostles, and we know how sadly in most cases it has failed. We know how empty speculation and vanity and pride have sprung up in such idle isolation, and how evil desires come more readily to the inactive watcher than to the busy worker. There is a rest and a heaven within which souls weary of the world may find, but it is discovered best in the world's midst, seeking its good and doing His will who lived and died to save it.

And then, last of all, watching without work is *unready for Christ*. The solitary watcher can have no works of faith nor labors of love to present, no saved souls to offer for the Redeemer's crown, and no crown of righteousness to receive from Him. He may be "looking for," but he is not "hasting unto," the coming of the day of God; standing with "his lamp burning," but not with "his loins girt." He is saved, but alone, as on a board or broken piece of the ship, not as they who have many voices of blessing around, and many welcomes before, and to whom an entrance is ministered abundantly into the everlasting kingdom of their Lord and Savior.

Let us see then the fitness of this union. "The Son of Man gave to every man his work, and commanded the porter to watch." What need of work! The world how dark—the soul how precious—time how short—life how irreparable—inquisition and judgment how stern! How much need of watching! How deceitful our hearts—how many our enemies—how insensibly slumber creeps on—how dreadful to be found sunk in carnal sleep in the breaking of the great day of God!

That man is happy who can combine them in perfect harmony—who has Stephen's life of labor and Stephen's vision in the end. In every soul there should be the sisters of Bethany, active effort and quiet thought, and both agreeing in mutual love and help. But Mary no longer sits at the feet of Christ and looks in His face; she stands at the door and gazes out into the open sky to watch the tokens of His coming, while in this hope her sister in the house still works. In due time He will be here to crown every humble effort with overflowing grace, to satisfy the longing soul that looks for Him, and to raise all the dead for whom we weep.

But what of those who neither work nor watch, who serve their own pleasure and forget that there is a coming hour which must give account of all? If there be any purpose in God's world, or truth in His book, or meaning in conscience, such an hour must arrive. "If the righteous scarcely be saved, where shall the ungodly and the sinner appear?" There is but one resource for any man—to grasp in faith the cross of Him who shall come on the throne. That cross disarms all the lightnings of His hand, for it finds an answer in His heart. To know it, live by it, serve under it, is true life now, and to look for its sign in the sky is the good hope, through grace, of life eternal.

# NOTES

## The Lord God Omnipotent Reigneth

**James S. Stewart** (1896-??) pastored three churches in Scotland before becoming professor of theology at the University of Edinburgh (1936) and then professor of New Testament (1946). But he is a professor who can preach, a scholar who can apply biblical truth to the needs of the common man, and a theologian who can make doctrine both practical and exciting. He has published several books of lectures and biblical studies, including *A Man in Christ* and *Heralds of God*. His two finest books of sermons are *The Gates of New Life* and *The Strong Name*.

This sermon was taken from *The Gates of New Life*, published in Edinburgh in 1939 by T. & T. Clark.

**James S. Stewart**

# 10

## THE LORD GOD OMNIPOTENT REIGNETH

Alleluia: for the Lord God omnipotent reigneth (Revelation 19:6).

WHAT IS THE BIGGEST FACT in life to you at this moment? What is the real center of your universe? "The biggest fact in life?" replies one man. "Well, I reckon it is my home. That, for me, is the center of everything." A very noble thing to be able to say! "A main fact in life to me," says a second, "is, without any shadow of doubt, my work. If you take that away from me, you take just everything." "The central thing for me," declares a third, "is health and happiness. As long as I have that, I am quite content. I can't bear to be unhappy." But what is your own answer?

I know what Jesus' answer was. Was it home? No—though none has ever hallowed home-life as Jesus hallowed it. Work, then? No—though none has toiled so terribly as the Son of God. Health and happiness? No—though none has been responsible for nearly so much clean happiness and mental and physical health as Jesus. The central fact in life to Jesus was none of these things. It was this—"the Lord God omnipotent reigneth!"

Is that your answer? More blessed than home, unspeakably blessed as home may be; more crucial than work, be that work never so urgent; more vital than health and happiness, though sometimes, especially when you lose them, happiness and health seem to be the only things that matter—greater and higher and deeper and more paramount than them all—the fact of God! The power behind every thought of your brain and every beat of your heart and every breath of your body—God! The element in which you live and move and have your being—God! The final, irreducible, and inescapable denominator of your universe—God! That was the conviction on which Christ staked His life and marched to Calvary; that is the conviction which can turn very ordinary people like ourselves into men and women of whom Christ and the saints will not need to be ashamed; this conviction, strong as steel, firm as a rock, and stirring as a battle-cry: "The Lord God omnipotent reigneth!"

Now that cardinal conviction will be found, when you explore and examine it, to lead to three results. It involves three tremendous consequences, and as these concern us all most intimately, I would ask you to think of them now.

### The Liberation of Life

It means, first, *the liberation of life*. It means a sense of absolute release. Release from what?

Release from petty worries, to begin with. Every one knows how sometimes things which are comparatively unimportant can obsess the mind and blot out all the sunshine. Here, let us say, is a man to whom some slight or some injustice has been administered, and he cannot get it out of his mind; he has not the grace to perform a surgical operation on that rankling thing, to cut it out and eradicate it; but he keeps on brooding and brooding about it, with his mind continually coming back to it, and going round it in wearisome circles—until the last vestige of peace of soul has been destroyed, his whole outlook on life warped, and all his sky obliterated by the mists and murky fogs of what is, from any spiritual standpoint, a wretched, insignificant triviality. Run and tell him, "The Lord God omnipotent reigneth!" Tell him to bring his worry into the light of that great truth, and just see how the fretting thing will fade and die. This, mark you, is not fancy nor hyperbole: it is proved experience, and the grace of the Lord Jesus Christ is in it.

The fact of the matter is, as Robert Browning said succintly, "'Tis looking downward that makes one dizzy." The man who has his gaze riveted on the narrow little circle of his own experience, obsessed (like the poor creature in Bunyan's dream) with the sticks and straws and dust of the floor, never thinking of the stars and the crown, cannot see life in true perspective. Oh, if only he would look away from all that—one long look into the face of the Lord God Almighty, if only he would take even five minutes in the morning to stabilize his soul by remembering Christ, how that would reinforce and liberate him! Yes, it is release—this great conviction—from the worries of life.

Notice, further, that it means release from the fears of life, and especially from the fear of tasks that seem too great for us. Life is forever trying to make us lose our nerve and turn away from new responsibilities, saying like Jeremiah, "I can't do this! You must let me off: I am not the man for it. Please, God, get someone else!" Do you know what it means, when you have some particularly difficult duty confronting you, to lie awake through the night, revolving your anxious fears? You have that dreadful three o'clock in the morning feeling, "I'll never get through this! I'll never be able for it." But if religion cannot help us there, there is something wrong.

I remember Dr. John Mott telling some of us of a conversation which he had had with Dr. Cheng, the great Christian leader in China. "Would it not be a great thing," said Dr. Cheng, "for all of us Christians in China to unite, and go out and double the number of Protestant Church Christians within the next five years?" Dr. Mott asked, "How many are there now?" "Four hundred and thirty-five thousand," was the answer. "Well," said Dr. Mott, "it has taken over a hundred years to build in China a Christian Church of these dimensions, and do you now suggest the practicability of doubling that number in five years?" And Mott said that never would he forget the answer. "Why not?" exclaimed that gallant Chinese leader. "Why not?" And indeed, when a man has seen God—*why not*? "Impossible?" cried Richard Cobden when they had been criticizing as wild and fanciful and quite unfeasible his agitation for the repeal of the Corn Laws, "Impossible? If that is all that is the matter, I move we go ahead!" And again—why not, if "the Lord God omnipotent reigneth"? It is release from the fears of life.

Moreover, it is release from self-contempt. One fact which modern psychology has been driving home to our minds is this, that there are multitudes of people today who are losing half the happiness which God intended them to have, and are being made quite unnecessarily miserable by inward repressions and conflicts and self-contemnings with which they do not know how to deal. And all the time there lies in religion (I am thinking, mark you, not of religion of the unbalanced, over-emotional, unduly introspective type, for that may easily do more harm than good, but of the sane, healthy, objective religion of Jesus of Nazareth) the power to end the conflict and to set the prisoned soul free. What is the key with which Christ's religion unlocks the prison door? What but this, "The Lord God omnipotent reigneth"? "There," declares Jesus, "is the Father of whom you—even you—are a son. Son of man, stand upon your feet! Son of the omnipotent God, lift up your head and be free!"

Release from worry, release from fear, release from self-contempt—all that is bound up with this great central conviction of the faith. It means the liberation of life.

## The Doom of Sin

But that is not all. Notice now, in the second place, that it means *the doom of sin*. It proclaims the ultimate defeat of evil in every shape and form.

Take this book of Revelation. You know the historic background of blood and smoke and martyrdom and reckless cynical laughter. Here you have the Rome of the Caesars and the Church of the Galilean locked in the death-grapple. Here you have the mailed fist of Nero and Domitian smashing its way through the hopes and dreams of the saints. Here you have, in the words of an old psalmist, "the kings of the earth taking counsel together against the Lord, and against His Anointed, saying, 'Let us break their bands asunder, and cast away their cords from us!'" Here you have the second Babylon, mother of all the abominations of the earth, drunk with the blood of the friends of Jesus, laughing in the intoxication of her triumph, shrieking with laughter to see the poor, pathetic Body of

Christ being crushed and mangled and battered out of existence. That is the background when this man takes up his pen to write. And you and I look over his shoulder, wondering what his message is going to be. What can it be, we think, but an elegy and a lament? "The battle is lost! Our cause is ruined. There is nothing left but to sue for mercy." Is that what we see him writing? No! But this—flinging defiance at all the facts, and with the ring of iron in it and the shout of the saints behind it—"Hallelujah! Babylon is fallen, is fallen!" And why? What made the man write like that? It was because at the back of the visible world, at the back of Caesar and all his pomp and pride, he had seen something which Caesar never saw, something which spelt the doom of Caesar and of all sin like Caesar's forever: a throne upreared above the earth, and on the throne the Lord God omnipotent reigning!

We sometimes talk pessimistically about the future of Christianity. We find ourselves wondering what will be the ultimate issue in the warfare between good and evil. Is it not possible that force and injustice may prevail, and that the Jesus whom we love may go down at last before the powers that are too strong for Him? But to anyone who has seen what this writer of Revelation saw, that is no longer an open question. Evil is done for—already. "Well," someone may say incredulously, "it certainly does not look like it. Look at the international scene. Look at our current literature. Look at the chaos in morals. See how evil flaunts itself in the open, how it strikes it roots deeper and still deeper." Yea, I know. But I know also this, that if God is on the throne of the universe, then evil is doomed, never has been anything else but doomed, doomed from the foundation of the world!

Now no one was ever so sure of this as Jesus. There was a day when the seventy followers whom He had sent out into the surrounding villages to preach and to heal returned to Him, with their faces eager and glowing and triumphant. "Master," they cried excitedly, "Master, it works—this new power that has been given to us—it really works! We have proved it. The darkest, foulest, most stubborn spirits are subject to us through Thy name!"

Whereupon, says the evangelist, Jesus, hearing that glad news, and realizing its deeper significance, which even they could not quite fathom, had a sudden vision. "I beheld Satan," He exclaimed, "as lightning fall from heaven!" as though to say—"This message which you have brought settles and confirms and ratifies My hope. The power of darkness is broken, snapped, done for; and henceforth the initiative is with God!"

Or take the amazing scene which meets you at the end. Have you not gazed in wonder at the sight of Christ before His judges? How calm and self-possessed He was, far more self-possessed than Caiaphas, or Pilate, or Herod, or any of the other actors on that tragic stage! What was the secret of it? Was it just His innate heroism asserting itself? Was it just Christ's way of steeling His heart to be brave? Was it only a reckless contempt of death? No. It was the open vision that behind Caiaphas, and behind Pilate, and behind Herod, there was Someone else; and that it was not they nor any earthly governor who reigned in Jerusalem that night, but that Other, that watching, brooding Figure among the shadows—God! And Caiaphas, Pilate, Herod—who or what were they? Less than the dust beneath time's chariot-wheels. The Lord God omnipotent reigneth!

Such was the source of Jesus' heroism. And such, in the face of all the evils of the world, has been the source of the blessed optimism of the saints in every age. God is on the throne: therefore evil is doomed. "Here on this Rock," said Jesus once, "I will build my Church, and the gates of hell shall not prevail against it." Here on the Rock! That sudden cry of Christ, echoing down into the world of darkness, must have shaken that world to its foundations—like the thunderous chant of a great marching host, fair as the moon, clear as the sun, terrible as an army with banners. Francis Xavier, four hundred years ago, said a magnificent thing about the Christian mission to the Far East. "You may be very sure of one thing," he declared, "the devil will be tremendously sorry to see the Company of the Name of Jesus enter China." And then he went on—"Just imagine! A thing so vile as I am to bring down such a vast reputation as the devil's! What great glory to God!" Do you ask what is the mainspring of Christian hope and courage? It is the certainty that we are not fighting a losing battle; that evil, flaunt itself as it may, carries the seal of its own doom upon it; and that the real pull of the universe is on the side of the man who goes out for righteousness.

Fight on, then, you who have lost heart because your own conflict is so difficult, your tempter so strong and dogged and subtle. Fight on! It is your battle, not his. For the Lord God omnipotent reigneth.

### The Comfort of Sorrow

We have seen, then, two decisive consequences bound up with our text: the liberation of life, and the doom of sin. I ask you, finally, to observe that we have here *the comfort of sorrow*.

The man who wrote the twenty-ninth psalm, which we wee reading today, had a marvelous sense of the dramatic. Do you remember how he sums up the great old story of the Flood in Genesis? He is looking back across the ages, and in imagination he can see that horror of the encroaching waters, rolling their waves higher and higher, creeping up with slow, inexorable destruction and death, and beating down all fragile human defenses built against them—until men and women, staring at those mounting waters, felt terror clutching at their throats, for the end of the world seemed nigh. All that, the psalmist sees; but he sees something else as well. "The Lord," he cries, "sat as King at the Flood." Then, like a great shout—"Yea, the Lord sitteth King forever!"

And what of the floods of life? What shall we say of the days which every soul must know when, as Jesus put it, "the rain descends, and the floods come, and the winds blow and beat upon the house," until your whole structure of things, all your philosophy of life, is threatening to come toppling down? What about the happiness you build for yourself—the plans you lay, the dreams you dream, the hopes you cherish, and the heart's desires you yearn for—and then, thundering and rolling mountain-high come the waves and the breakers, crashing down on that shore of dreams, leaving only some poor bits of wreckage behind? What then? Why then, blessed be God, the Lord sits as King at the flood, and the Lord sitteth King forever! Which simply means that the heartbreaking things of life have meaning and purpose and grace in them, for the Lord God omnipotent reigneth.

There was a terrible night out on the Galilean Lake when the sudden whirlwind blew, and the sea was lashed to fury, and the boat struggled in the troughs of the waves, and the disciples were telling themselves—"Our last hour has come: this is the end!" And there was Jesus, sleeping through it all. "Master, Master, careth Thou not that we perish?" But that night they learned by the grace of God this lesson—that there is something higher in human experience than life's waves and storms: there is a Christ who rules the waves! Have we discovered that? It is a great thing, when the floods begin and the desolation of sorrow comes beating down, to hear the divine sursum *corda*—up with your heart!—for the Lord sits King at the flood, your flood, and the Lord God omnipotent reigneth!

Did not Chesterton, in one of his most vivid poems, preach the same victory of the soul? "Though giant rains put out the sun, Here stand I for a sign. Though Earth be filled with waters dark, My cup is filled with wine. Tell to the trembling priests that here Under the deluge rod, One nameless, tattered, broken man Stood up and drank to God."

There was once a flood called Calvary. And all the bitterness and ugliness, all the shame and sorrow of life, entered into that flood, and came beating around the brave soul of Jesus, sweeping Him down at last to the barbarity and infamy of the death of the cross. "What can God have been doing?" we want to ask. "Was He asleep? Or on a journey? Or was He dead?" No! The Lord was sitting as King at the flood, that surging flood of Calvary; and out of that grim cross He has brought the salvation of the world. Tell me—if God did that with the cross of Jesus, do you think your cross can be too difficult for Him to deal with, and to transfigure? He can make it shine with glory.

Do you believe it? My friend, here is surely the final victory of faith—to be able to say, "The Lord God omnipotent reigneth," to cry it aloud, not only when life is kind and tender and smiling, and the time of the singing of birds is come and flowers appear on the earth, but even more when the night is dark, and you are far from home, and the proud waters are going over your soul; to cry it then, not weakly nor diffidently nor uncertainly, but vehemently and passionately and with the ring of faith in every syllable of it—"The Lord God omnipotent reigneth. Hallelujah!"

This is the Lord God who has come again to the gate of your life and mine today. This is the Lord God who claims the right to reign, and from whose patient, haunting pursuit we can never in this world get free. Behold, He stands at the door, and knocks. While the sands of time are running out and the hurrying days mold our destiny, He stands at the door and knocks. Tenderer than the kiss of a little child, mightier than the flashing lightnings of Heaven, He stands at the door and knocks. What will our answer be? "You, out there at the door, you who have been haunting and troubling me all these years—begone, and leave me in peace!" Is that it? Or is it not rather this? "Blessed and glorious Lord Almighty, dear loving Christ of God—come! Come now. My life is yours. See, here is the throne. Oh, Christ, take your power—and reign!"

## The Second Coming of Christ

**Dwight Lyman Moody** (1837-1899) is known around the world as one of America's most effective evangelists. Converted as a teenager through the witness of his Sunday School teacher, Moody became active in YMCA and Sunday School work in Chicago while pursuing a successful business career. He then devoted his full time to evangelism and was mightily used of God in campaigns in both the United States and Great Britain. He founded the Northfield School for Girls, the Mount Hermon School for Boys, the Northfield Bible Conference, and the Moody Bible Institute in Chicago. Before the days of planes and radio, Moody traveled more than a million miles and addressed more than 100 million people.

This message is from *The Gospel Awakening*, edited by L. T. Remlap, and published in 1879 by J. Fairbanks and Company, Chicago.

**Dwight Lyman Moody**

# 11

# THE SECOND COMING OF CHRIST

YOU THAT HAVE BEEN here the last three Sunday mornings remember that I have been talking about Christ. Three weeks ago, this morning, we were looking at Christ in the Old Testament, and how the prophecy was fulfilled in regard to His coming; and the next Sabbath we were talking about His birth: and last Sunday of John, the forerunner to introduce Him; and you remember that I have spoken here, during the last three months, of His birth, His life, His miracles, His parables, His death, His burial, His resurrection and His ascension. Now, this morning I want to talk about His coming again. (A voice: "Amen!") There is more said in the Epistles about the Lord Jesus Christ returning to this earth than there is about baptism. There is no denomination, no church scarcely, but that lays great stress upon that order; and God forbid that I should say anything that would give you to understand that I look upon it lightly. I think that every order that the Lord has given us, and ever commanded us to do, ought to be carried out literally; but we find that this doctrine has been, as it were, laid aside by the churches sometimes—they have forgotten all about it. But I don't know anything that will quicken of our Lord's return. (A voice: "Amen!") If I read my Bible correctly, in the Epistles baptism is referred to thirteen times and the Lord's return upward of fifty times. So that it is not an unscriptural idea that I want to bring before you this morning. If the Word of God doesn't teach it, my friends, don't you receive it; but let us be ready and willing to bow to Scripture, because we read that all Scriptures are given by inspiration; that we are not to be one-sided Christians, and take up one truth and harp on that all the time; but we are to take up the whole Word of God.

Just turn to the 2 Peter 1:19: "We have also a more sure word of prophecy; whereunto ye do well that ye take heed, as unto a light that shineth in a dark place, until the day dawn, and the day-star arise in your hearts: Knowing this first, that no prophecy of the Scripture is of any private interpretation." No private interpretation. It is for the whole Church of God—the whole family of God. "For the prophecy came not in old time by the will of man; but holy men of God spake as they were moved by the Holy Spirit."

Now you know Gabriel came down to announce the conception of Christ, and angels came to announce His birth: angels came to announce His resurrection; angels came to announce His return. When those apostles stood there gazing up into heaven, two angels dropped down there. "And it came to pass, as they were much perplexed thereabout, behold, two men stood by them in shining garments. And as they were afraid, and bowed down their faces to the earth, they said unto them: 'Why seek ye the living among the dead? He is not here, but is risen; remember how he spake unto you when he was yet in Galilee, saying, The Son of man must be delivered into the hands of sinful men, and be crucified, and the third day rise again.'" Yes, thank God, He is coming again, just as He went. (A voice: "Amen!") We are going to see Him in person; He that left this world blessing it—for that is the way He left this world, blessing it—is coming back to bless His own church and to receive them that have waited for His return. If you read the 26th chapter of Matthew, the 64th verse, you will find that it was just this very thing that caused His death. When the high priests asked Him who He was, and if He was the true Messiah, what does He say: "Jesus saith unto him, Thou hast said: nevertheless I say unto you, Hereafter shall ye see the clouds of heaven." That was enough. The moment they heard that, they accused him of blasphemy and condemned Him to death, just because He said He was coming again. "Ye shall see me coming in the clouds of glory."

**The Time of His Coming**

Now, let me say that this doctrine has suffered a good deal from those who claim to be its friends, because they set a time—a certain day—for His coming. Now, we read here in Matthew 24:36 that no man knows when He shall come. "But of that day and hour knoweth no man, no, not the angels of heaven, but my Father only." It seems to me that the devil is all the time trying to counterfeit these precious truths, so that the mass of Christians will not believe it. Now, there it is clearly taught that the day and the hour knoweth no man, no, not the angels in heaven. Now, when a man comes and tells you that he knows when Christ is coming—that He is coming next year, or in any particular year or at any particular time, he has got no truth for that assertion. "The day and the hour knoweth no man." I think if we knew the day and the hour of His coming, we wouldn't be watching for His coming. All through the Scriptures we are told to watch for His coming.

"Therefore be ye also ready, for in such an hour as ye think not the Son of man cometh." And then we are also taught that His coming shall be sudden. We find in Matthew 24:37-39: "But as the days of Noe were, so shall also the coming of the Son of man be." "For as in the days that were before the flood they were eating and drinking, marrying and giving in marriage, until the day that Noe entered the ark. And knew not until the flood came and took them all away; so shall also the coming of the Son of man be." Now, we have that order that the time of His coming is unknown; that He is coming unexpectedly. He is coming suddenly; but let us bear in mind that He is coming, because that word has gone out.

Now, I can imagine some of you say, "He is coming to us when we die." But that is not what is taught here. Death is not the coming of the Lord. Just turn to John 21:18-19: "Verily, verily, I say unto thee, When thou wast young, thou girdest thyself, and walkedst whither thou wouldst; but when thou shalt behold, thou shalt stretch forth thy hands, and another shall gird thee, and carry thee whither thou wouldest not. This spake he, signifying by what death he should glorify God. And when he had spoken this, he saith unto him, Follow me." Now, the thought I want to call your attention to is this; that Christ didn't look to His death and His coming as one and the same thing. He kept them distinct. His coming is one thing; His death is another. You and I may be summoned away before Christ comes; but I am not taught anywhere in the Scripture to look for death. That is not in the Scripture. We are told to look for the coming of the Lord. Now, Peter wanted to know what John should do. "Jesus saith unto him, If I will that he tarry till I come, what is that to thee? follow thou me." That is, you are to follow Me, and not look to see what this disciple or that disciple is going to do. "Then went this saying abroad among the brethren, that the disciple should not die; yet Jesus said not unto him, he shall not die; but, If I will that he tarry till I come, what is that to thee?" There is a difference between death and His coming. Now, I think that we make a great mistake in saying that death is the coming of the Lord. Death is one thing; and the coming of the Lord is another. Why, the year of jubilee will burst upon this world by and by; and we shall come up out of our graves. That is distinct and separate from death. It will be all life then. We shall be changed in the twinkling of an eye. Enoch was one type of life, He was caught up into heaven. Elijah was translated from earth to heaven, in a fiery chariot. These two represented the first two dispensations; and so Christ, who represented the third, has gone up; and when He comes these bodies shall come forth from their graves. We are not going to die. If the world remains, if we wait until Christ comes, we are going to defy death. Death has been conquered, and by and by, I don't know when, in the fullness of time, we shall rise victorious to glory. He shall come and set up His kingdom on earth. As we read in the prophecy of Daniel, that stone cut out of the mountains without hands is growing, and it is going to fill the whole earth. God has decreed it.

## The Nature of His Coming

Now, I think it is decreed in Thessalonians, and if you have your Bibles, here I should like to have you turn to Thessalonians, because this passage is written, just as it were, to the young converts. Every chapter in that first Epistle is a sermon to young converts about His coming. "For the Lord himself shall descend from heaven with a shout, with the voice of the archangel, and with the trump of God; and the dead in Christ shall rise first; Then we which are alive and remain shall be caught up together with them in the clouds to meet the Lord in the air; and so shall we ever be with the Lord. Wherefore comfort one another with these words." That is the comfort of the church; not that we are going to die, but that the Lord may come at any time and take us away into that bridal chamber. Now, it is said that His coming in judgment on the earth to dash the nations to pieces that have disobeyed Him, is one coming, and that His coming to take His bride away is altogether different. So His first coming is in the air; and that is when we shall be caught up to meet the Lord in the air. "For the Lord himself shall descend from heaven with a shout, with the voice of the archangel, and with the trump of God; and the dead in Christ shall rise first." Then, over here, in John 5:25-29, "Verily, verily, I say unto you. The hour is coming, and now is, when the dead shall hear the voice of the Son of God; and they that hear shall live. For as the Father hath life in himself; so hath he given to the Son to have life in himself. And hath given him authority to execute judgment also, because He is the Son of man. Marvel not at this, for the hour is coming, in which all that are in their graves shall hear his voice. and shall come forth."

And by and by these slumbering bodies shall be awakened by the trump of God; and they shall come forth from their graves, and fly to meet the King of Glory. "And they shall come forth, they that have done good, unto the resurrection of life; and they that have done evil, unto the resurrection of damnation." Now, you take a strong piece of magnet, and then have little pieces of iron or steel, mixed up in some sawdust; and just hold that magnet over it. Every particle of steel and iron will fly to meet that magnet. So when He shall come upon the earth, every one of His chosen shall fly to meet Him. The hour is coming when the trump shall sound; the Lord of Hosts shall come. Oh, Christ is going to come. Let us be waiting and watching and praying that He may come quickly.

Now, there are three great facts taught in Scripture. First, that Christ is coming again. The next, that the Holy Spirit was to come on us here, in the world. Now, do you believe that this assembly would have been drawn together for the past three months, if it had not been for the power of the Holy Spirit? Do you believe that men would have been converted, if it had not been for the power of the Holy Spirit. Is there any eloquence, any power in man that can turn the whole current of men's lives; that can transform a poor, miserable drunkard, one who has made his home a hell, who has beaten and abused his wife. Can any eloquence, any power in man, I say, do that unless it is by and through the power of the Holy Spirit? The next great fact that this Bible teaches is, that He is coming again. What is it that makes John 14 so sweet? You know there is probably not a chapter in the whole Bible that is read so much as that one in John. What makes it so sweet? why, because it tells us He shall come again. "Let not your hearts be troubled; ye believe in God; believe also in me. In my Father's house are many mansions; if it were not so I would have told you. I go to prepare a place for you." Then what does He say? "And if I go and prepare a place for you I will come again and receive you unto myself, that where I am there ye may be also." That is the key-note to John 14—not that He is coming Himself. He Himself is coming back after His bride. He came down here to get a bride, and the world rose up and cast Him out and said He shouldn't have a bride. Then He went up above, and has been there these 1800 years gathering out His bride. Some one says, you can get some idea of how magnificent these mansions are by the time He takes to get them built.

## Watching for His Coming

Now, there is no place in the Scripture where we are told to watch for signs—the rebuilding of Babylon, or the returning of the Jews to Jerusalem; but all through Scripture we are told what to do—just to watch for Him; just to be waiting for our Lord's return from heaven. In Paul's Epistle to the Philippians we read: "For our conversion is in heaven; from whence also we look for the Savior, the Lord Jesus Christ: who shall change our vile body, that it may be fashioned like unto his glorious body, according to the working whereby he is able even to subdue all things unto himself." "Looking for our Lord and Savior." And that's the attitude of every true believer in this world, with loins girded, lamps trimmed and burning, all watching for the coming of the Bridegroom. Thank God, He will say when Christ comes, "Behold, the bridegroom cometh." Now, He says again here, in Titus 2:13: "Looking for that blessed hope, and the glorious appearing of the great God and our Savior Jesus Christ."

Now, if you will just take your Bibles, a great many of you will find that, over and over again, the Lord has said that we are to be waiting and watching for His coming. The last prayer in Scripture—what is it? "Come quickly, Lord Jesus." And that ought to be the cry of every child of God: "Come quickly, Lord Jesus." Think of the war that is bursting upon the nations across the waters. Think of the blood and carnage. Think of the widows and orphan children, of the suffering that is going to be in those nations. But, thank God, when He comes there will be no more war. (A voice: "Amen!") There will be no more suffering. There will be peace. Then, in Mark 13:32-37 it says: "But of that day and that hour knoweth no man, no, not the angels which are in heaven, neither the Son, but the Father. Take ye heed, watch and pray for ye know not when the time is. For the Son of man is like a man taking a far journey, who left his house, and gave authority to his servants, and to every man his work, and commanded the porter to watch. Watch ye therefore, for ye know not when the Master of the house cometh, at even, or at midnight, or at the cockcrowing, or in the morning. Lest coming suddenly he find you sleeping. And what I say unto you I say unto all, Watch." He may come in the morning; He may come in the evening; He may come at the cockcrowing. In another place, Luke 17, it says: "Two women shall be grinding together; the one shall be taken and the other left. Two men shall be in the field; the one shall be taken and the other left." Christ is going to take out His chosen from among the scoffers. By and by, He is going to separate His children, and the scoffers and the workers of iniquity. They may scoff and laugh now; but I tell you, by and by, there will be nothing left of them. My friends, you will find it to be true that every portion of the Old Testament referring to Christ's coming has been fulfilled. Now, people say this is so wonderful, so beyond all reason, so beyond all common sense that we cannot lay hold of it. Now, His second coming cannot be so wonderful as His first coming. If a man had stood up and said that Christ was going to be born of a virgin; that He was going to be laid in a manger; that He was going to be the son of a carpenter, and going to work at the carpenter's trade Himself (as He did), there wouldn't have been a man in the world who would have believed him. "Oh, that is figurative," they would have said. And that's just the way men talk now, and just figure away everything. The Scripture was literally fulfilled. He came, just the way that the prophets said He would come; and once, as I said the other morning, He had to ride into Jerusalem, because it was prophesied that He should. Everything was fulfilled. Now, this prophecy in the New Testament about His coming, in my mind, my friends, I haven't the slightest doubt but that it is going to be fulfilled. That same Jesus that was crucified at Mount Calvary, we shall see at Mount Calvary again—see His hands and His feet pierced with the nails, and it is a question in my mind whether the Jews will not receive Him when He comes back. They will receive Him as the true Messiah, and take up the glorious news of the coming of the Messiah, and spread it around the world.

A great many say: "This doctrine of the second coming

of Christ cannot affect me. He can't come in my day. A great many things have got to take place before He comes. The thousand years of the millennium have got to come before He does." That is just the way I used to talk. "Why," I used to say, "He can't come in my day. Don't you know that there is to be one thousand years of the millennium; that righteousness must increase and wickedness must decrease before He comes?" Ah, my friends, but since I have got a little better acquainted with the Word of God, I find that is not God's plan; that is not what is taught here. Why, just see what He says: "This know also, that in the last days perilous times shall come." That doesn't sound like the millennium, does it? "For men shall be lovers of their own selves, covetous, boasters, proud, blasphemers, disobedient to parents, unthankful, unholy." "Boasters." There is some boasting done here in Boston. "Without natural affection, truce-breakers, false accusers, incontinent, fierce, despisers of those that are good. Traitors, heady, high-minded, lovers of pleasure more than lovers of God." I think we are coming pretty near those days now. "Having a form of godliness, but denying the power thereof; from such turn away. For of this sort are they which creep into houses, and lead captive silly women laden with sins, led away with divers lusts, ever learning, and never able to come to the knowledge of the truth. But they shall proceed no further, for their folly shall be manifest unto all men, as theirs also was. But thou hast fully known my doctrine, manner of life, purpose, faith, long-suffering, charity, patience. Persecutions, afflictions, which came unto me at Antioch, at Iconium, at Lystra, what persecutions I endured; but out of them all the Lord delivered me. Yea, and all that will live godly in Christ Jesus shall suffer persecution. But evil men and seducers shall wax worse and worse, deceiving and being deceived."

The fact is, my friends, the world is going to destruction; and what God wants is to have us come out from it. "Wherefore come out from among them, and be ye separate, saith the Lord, and touch not the unclean thing; and I will receive you. And will be a Father unto you, and ye shall be my sons and daughters, saith the Lord Almighty.

Having therefore these promises, dearly beloved, let us cleanse ourselves from all filthiness of the flesh and spirit, perfecting holiness in the fear of God." And He is not redeeming His children, taking them out from the world; and the sons of Light ought to grow stronger and stronger; but the wicked men are waxing worse and worse.

When we read over here about the coming of the Son of God, that it shall be as in the days of Noah. How was it then? Were men then praising God, living for God's glory? Just see what it says: "But as the days of Noe were, so shall also the coming of the Son of Man be. For as in the days that were before the flood, they were eating and drinking, marrying and giving in marriage, until the day that Noe entered into the ark. And knew not until the flood came, and took them all away; so shall also the coming of the Son of Man be." There will be drunkenness in the world when He comes. Don't flatter yourselves, my dear friends, that the world is going to be better and better. The world has not got better. It may be that the children of God are getting stronger and stronger; but this world is like a wrecked vessel. It is going to pieces on the rocks, and God wants you to do everything you can to rescue your souls. Now, some people say, "O don't preach that! You will drive away people by preaching that doctrine." I don't know of anything that will quicken men; I don't know of anything that will take the men of this world out of their bonds and stocks quicker than that our Lord is coming again. The way it looks to me is this: Here is a vessel going to pieces on the rocks. God puts a lifeboat in my hands, and says: "Rescue every man you can. Get them out of this wrecked vessel." So God wants us to get our family out of the wrecked world into the ark of safety, as Noah did his family, and have them in Christ; and if they are in Christ, they are safe.

Let me call your attention to 2 Peter 3:3-4: "Knowing this first, that there shall come in the last days scoffers, walking after their own lusts, and saying, Where is the promise of his coming? for since the fathers fell asleep, all things continue as they were from the beginning of the creation." Are we not just living in those days? Just look at the scoffer saying, "Where is the promise of his coming? Everything is moving on. The sun, moon and stars are shining just the same as they have been from the creation. Where is the promise of His coming? Why, we are going on to perfection! Everything is growing better and better." But that isn't what this Word teaches. It teaches that the heavens shall roll up like a scroll. He wants us to get into Christ, and if we are in Him we are saved. Just turn to Matthew 24:48-51: "But, and if that evil servant shall say in his heart, my lord delayeth his coming; and shall begin to smite his fellow-servants, and to eat and drink with the drunken; the lord of that servant shall come in a day when he looketh not for him, and in an hour that he is not aware of; and shall cut him asunder, and appoint him his portion with the hypocrites; there shall be weeping and gnashing of teeth."

There is another warning. I have only time to just touch on this wonderful subject. The Bible is full of them. I want to urge these young converts to begin and study the whole Word of God. I don't want them to be hoggish, and take up one part only, but the whole Word of God; so that at these times you may know just what you are to receive and what you are to reject, and that you have got a reason for the hope that is within you.

Now I want to call your attention to another thing; that is, that every time you go to the Lord's table, you will go there not only to show forth His death, but what else? "For as often as ye eat this bread and drink this cup, ye do show the Lord's death till he come." How many that go to the Lord's table ever think of His return? Now, I will tell you where men make a great mistake. They go to the Lord's table with dread. I used to dread communion Sundays—a week from this Sunday, I am told, is communion Sunday. I used to dread it. We used to have it once in three months. Now it is once a month; and I hope we will have it every Sabbath. I used to go there thinking of my own sins, and the short-comings of the committee; and it was most unpleasant. But I found out that I was to go there to remember Him; and now it is a place of rejoicing. I try to think just as little of myself when I go to the

Lord's table as I can. There isn't any place in Scripture where you are told to examine yourselves when you go there; but you are to go there to remember the Lord, and that He is coming back again. That is what we are to think about. We are to think of His death until He comes.

But then I can imagine that some of you say that, if I preach this doctrine, that the world is going to be destroyed, that grace has been a failure. Now let me say, right here, that grace has not been a failure. Man has failed to lay hold of it; and the world has spurned the Word of God, just as the Jews did Christ, years ago. They would not receive Him. Now, the grace of God is over all the world, and the world has rejected it. Thank God, here and there is one that will lay hold of it; and if men won't take hold of it, they ought not to complain that God is going to punish them for it. Because, when He sent His prophets, they killed them; they crucified His Son, and would not receive the Holy Spirit; and they trampled His Word under their feet. Why, you cannot say He is unjust. If a man says, "I hate the grace of God, the gift of God; I don't want the salvation of God through Jesus Christ"; if a man wants to be excused from the marriage feast of the Lamb, why, don't go off and say grace has been a failure; but they have failed to lay hold of it.

Now, there is another thing; that when Christ comes we are going to be reunited with our loved ones. There are a good many here in this congregation that have more friends in heaven than on earth. Some of you mothers have more children there than down here. Yes, there is a better day for us, my friends. Glory and honor to God; Christ is coming back; and I am going to see my loved ones again. I am just waiting and watching for the hour when I shall hear that trump sound; and I shall be released to meet those loved ones; and those that are with me, that are in Christ, shall go up together, and we shall be forever with the Lord. Oh, how we ought to hail that day, and how the church ought to be watching! Oh, that God would wean us from the world, that we should not have our hearts set on things down here, but on things above, where Christ is.

I want to call your attention to a few passages of Scripture. In 1 Corinthians 11:25-26, it says: "After the same manner also he took the cup, when he had supped, saying, This cup is the New Testament in my blood: this do ye, as oft as ye drink it, in remembrance of me. For as often as ye eat this bread, and drink this cup, ye do shew the Lord's death till he come." In Luke 19:13 He tells us to use our talents until He comes. We must fight the good fight of faith until He comes. "And he called his ten servants, and delivered them ten pounds, and said unto them, Occupy till I come." In 1 Timothy 6:12-14: "Fight the good fight of faith, lay hold on eternal life, whereunto thou art also called, and hast professed a good profession before many witnesses. I give thee charge in the sight of God, who quickeneth all things, and before Christ Jesus, who before Pontius Pilate witnessed a good confession. That thou keep this commandment without spot, unrebukable, until the appearing of our Lord Jesus Christ." In 2 Thessalonians 1:7: "And to you who are troubled, rest with us, when the Lord Jesus shall be revealed from heaven with his mighty angels." In James 5:8: "Be ye also patient; establish your hearts; for the coming of the Lord draweth nigh." In 2 Timothy 4:8, we are to wait for the crown of righteousness: Henceforth there is laid up for me a crown of righteousness, which the Lord, the righteous judge, shall give me at that day; and not to me only, but unto them also that love his appearing." In 1 Timothy 2:5-8: "For there is one God, and one mediator between God and men, the man Jesus Christ; who gave himself a ransom for all to be testified in due time. Whereunto I am ordained a preacher, and an apostle, (I speak the truth in Christ, and lie not;) a teacher of the Gentiles in faith and verity."

"I will therefore that men pray everywhere, lifting up holy hands, without wrath and doubting." In 1 Thessalonians 4:13-18: "But I would not have you to be ignorant brethren, concerning them which are asleep, that ye sorrow not, even as others which have no hope. For if we believe that Jesus died and rose again, even so them also which sleep in Jesus will God bring with him. For this we say unto you by the word of the Lord, that we which are alive and remain unto the coming of the Lord shall not prevent them which are asleep. For the Lord Himself shall descend from heaven with a shout, with the voice of the archangel and the trump of God; and the dead in Christ shall rise first. Then we which are alive and remain shall be caught up together with them in the clouds to meet the Lord in the air; and so shall we ever be with the Lord. Wherefore comfort one another with these words."

We are to wait for Satan to be bound until He comes. Oh, he's going to be bound that day, and Christ, who has a right to take the throne of David, is going to take it. Let us pray that He may come quickly. Let that be the burden of our prayers.

# NOTES

## The Great Assize

**John Wesley** (1703-1781), along with his brother Charles, and George Whitefield, founded the Methodist movement in Britain and America. On May 24, 1738, he had his great spiritual experience in a meeting at Aldersgate Street, when his "heart was strangely warmed" and he received assurance of salvation. Encouraged by Whitefield to do open-air preaching, Wesley soon was addressing thousands, in spite of the fact that many churches were closed to him. The Methodist "societies" he formed became local churches that conserved the results of his evangelism. He wrote many books and preached 40,000 sermons during his long ministry.

This one is taken from *Works of John Wesley*, volume 5, published by Zondervan and was preached in Bedford, England, March 10, 1758.

John Wesley

# 12

## THE GREAT ASSIZE

We shall all stand before the judgment seat of Christ (Romans 14:10).

1. How many circumstances concur to raise the awfulness of the present solemnity!—The general *concourse* of people of every age, sex, rank, and condition of life, willingly or unwillingly gathered together, not only from the neighboring, but from distant parts; *criminals*, speedily to be brought forth, and having no way to escape; *officers*, waiting in their various posts, to execute the orders which shall be given; and the *representative* of our gracious *Sovereign*, whom we so highly reverence and honor. The *occasion* likewise of this assembly adds not a little to the solemnity of it: To hear the determined causes of every kind, some of which are of the most important nature; on which depends no less than life or death, death that uncovers the face of eternity! It was, doubtless, in order to increase the serious sense of these things, and not in the minds of the vulgar only, that wisdom of our forefathers did not disdain to appoint even several minute circumstances of this solemnity. For these also, by means of the eye or ear, may more deeply affect the heart: And when viewed in this light, trumpets, staves, apparel, are no longer trifling or insignificant, but subservient, in their kind and degree, to the most valuable ends of society.

2. But, as awful as this solemnity is, one far more awful is at hand. For yet a little while, and "we shall all stand before the judgment seat of Christ." "For, as I live, saith the Lord; every knee shall bow to me, and every tongue shall confess to God." And in that day, "every one of us shall give account of himself to God."

3. Had all men a deep sense of this, how effectually would it secure the interests of society! For what more

forcible motive can be conceived to the practice of genuine morality? to a steady pursuit of solid virtue? and uniform walking in justice, mercy, and truth? What could strengthen our hands in all that is good, and deter us from all evil, like a strong conviction of this, "The Judge standeth at the door"; and we are shortly to stand before Him?

4. It may not therefore be improper, or unsuitable to the design of the present assembly, to consider,

I. The chief circumstances which will precede our standing before the judgment seat of Christ;
II. The judgment itself; and,
III. A few of the circumstances which will follow it.

## The Chief Circumstances

I. 1. Let us, in the first place, consider the chief circumstances which will precede our standing before the judgment seat of Christ.

And, first, God will show "signs in the earth beneath" (Acts 2:19); particularly He will "arise to shake terribly the earth." "The earth shall reel to and fro like a drunkard, and shall be removed like a cottage" (Isa. 24:20). "There shall be earthquakes," (not in divers only, but) "in *all* places;" not in one only, or a few, but in every part of the habitable world (Luke 21:11); even "such as were not since men were upon the earth, so mighty earthquakes and so great." In one of these "every island shall flee away, and the mountains will not be found" (Rev. 16:20).

Meantime all the waters of the terraqueous globe will feel the violence of those concussions; "the sea and waves roaring" (Luke 21:25), with such agitation as had never been known before, since the hour that "the fountains of the great deep were broken up," to destroy the earth, which then "stood out of the water and in the water." The air will be all storm and tempest, full of dark vapors and pillars of smoke (Joel 2:30); resounding with thunder from pole to pole, and torn with ten thousand lightnings. But the commotion will not stop in the region of the air; "the powers of heaven also shall be shaken. There shall be signs in the sun, and in the moon, and in the stars" (Luke

21:25,26); those fixed, as well as those that move round them. "The sun be turned into darkness, and the moon into blood, before the great and terrible day of the Lord come" (Joel 2:31). "The stars shall withdraw their shining" (Joel 3:15), yea, and "fall from heaven" (Rev. 6:13), being thrown out of their orbits. And then shall be heard the universal *shout*, from all the companies of heaven, followed by the "voice of the archangel," proclaiming the approach of the Son of God and Man, "and the trumpet of God," sounding an alarm to all that sleep in the dust of the earth (1 Thess. 4:16). In consequences of this, all the graves shall open, and the bodies of men arise. The sea also shall give up the dead which are therein (Rev. 20:13), and every one shall rise with "his own body"; his own in substance, although so changed in its properties as we cannot now conceive. "For this corruptible will" then "put on incorruption, and this mortal put on immortality" (1 Cor. 15:53). Yea, "death, and hades," the invisible world, shall "deliver up the dead that are in them" (Rev. 20:13). So that all who ever lived and died, since God created man, shall be raised incorruptible and immortal.

2. At the same time, "the Son of man shall send forth his angels" over all the earth; and they shall "gather his elect from the four winds, from one end of heaven to the other" (Matt. 24:31). And the Lord Himself shall come with clouds, in His own glory, and the glory of His Father, with ten thousand of His saints, even myriads of angels, and shall sit upon the throne of His glory. "And before him shall be gathered all nations, and he shall separate them one from another, and shall set the sheep," the good, "on his right hand, and the goats," the wicked, "upon the left" (Matt. 25:31, etc.). Concerning this general assembly it is, that the beloved disciple speaks thus: "I saw the dead," all that had been dead, "small and great, stand before God. And the books were opened" (a figurative expression, plainly referring to the manner of proceeding among men), "and the dead were judged out of those things which were written in the books, according to their works" (Rev. 20:12).

II. These are the chief circumstances which are recorded in the oracles of God, as preceding the general judgment. We are, secondly, to consider the judgment itself, so far as it hath pleased God to reveal it.

1. The person by whom God will judge the world is His only-begotten Son, whose "goings forth are from everlasting"; "who is God over all, blessed forever." Unto Him, being "the outbeaming of his Father's glory, the express image of his person" (Heb. 1:3), the Father "hath committed all judgment, because he is the Son of Man" (John 5:22, 27); because, though He was "in the form of God, and thought it not robbery to be equal with God, yet he emptied himself, taking upon him the form of a servant, being made in the likeness of men" (Phil. 2:6,7); yea, because, "being found in fashion as a man, he humbled himself" yet farther, "becoming obedient unto death, even the death of the cross. Wherefore God hath highly exalted him," even in his human nature, and "ordained him," as man, to try the children of men, "to be the Judge both of the quick and dead"; both of those who shall be found alive at His coming, and of those who were before gathered to their fathers.

2. The time termed by the Prophet, "The great and the terrible day," is usually, in Scripture, styled, *the day of the Lord*. The space from the creation of man upon the earth, to the end of all things, is *the day of the sons of men*; the time that is now passing over us is properly *our day*; when this is ended, *the day of the Lord* will begin. But who can say how long it will continue? "With the Lord one day is as a thousand years, and a thousand years as one day" (2 Peter 3:8). And from this very expression, some of the ancient Fathers drew that inference, that what is commonly called the day of judgment would be indeed a thousand years: And it seems they did not go beyond the truth; nay, probably they did not come up to it. For, if we consider the number of persons who are to be judged, and of actions which are to be inquired into, it does not appear that a thousand years will suffice for the transactions of that day; so that it may not improbably comprise several thousand years. But God shall reveal this also in its season.

3. With regard to the place where mankind will be

judged, we have no explicit account in Scripture. An eminent writer (but not he alone; many have been of the same opinion) supposes it will be on earth, where the works were done, according to which they shall be judged; and that God will, in order thereto, employ the angels of His strength:

> To smooth and lengthen out the boundless space,
> And spread an area for all human race.

But perhaps it is more agreeable to our Lord's own account of His coming in the clouds, to suppose it will be above the earth, if not "twice a planetary height." And this supposition is not a little favored by what St. Paul writes to the Thessalonians: "The dead in Christ shall rise first. Then we who remain alive, shall be caught up together with them, in the clouds, to meet the Lord in the air" (1 Thess. 4:16,17). So that it seems most probable, the great white throne will be high exalted above the earth.

### The Judgment Itself

4. The persons to be judged, who can count, any more than the drops of rain, or the sands of the sea? "I beheld," saith St. John, "a great multitude which no man can number, clothed with white robes, and palms in their hands." How immense then must be the total multitude of all nations, and kindreds, and people, and tongues; of all that have sprung from the loins of Adam, since the world began, till time shall be no more! If we admit the common supposition, which seems no ways absurd, that the earth bears, at any one time, no less than four hundred millions of living souls, men, women, and children; what a congregation must all those generations make who have succeeded each other for seven thousand years!

> Great Xerxes' world arms, proud Cannae's host,
> They all are here; and here they all are lost.
> Their numbers swell to be discern'd in vain;
> Lost as a drop in the unbounded main.

Every man, every woman, every infant of days, that

ever breathed the vital air, will then hear the voice of the Son of God, and start into life, and appear before Him. And this seems to be the natural import of that expression, "the dead, small and great" All universally, all without exception, all of every age, sex, or degree; all that ever lived and died, or underwent such a change as will be equivalent with death, that vanishes away. Who is rich or great in the grave?

5. And every man shall there "give an account of his own works"; yea, a full and true account of all that he ever did while in the body, whether it was good or evil. O what a scene will then be disclosed, in the sight of angels and men!—while not the fabled Rhadamanthus, but the Lord God Almighty, who knoweth all things in heaven and in earth:

> O'er these drear realms stern Rhadamanthus reigns,
> Detects each artful villain, and constrains
> To own the crimes long veil'd from human sight:
> In vain! Now all stand forth in hated light.

Nor will the actions alone of every child of man be then brought to open view, but all their words; seeing "every idle word which men shall speak, they shall give account thereof in the day of judgment" (Matt. 12:36,37); so that "by thy words," as well as works, "thou shalt be justified; or by thy words thou shalt be condemned." Will not God then bring to light every circumstance also, that accompanied every word or action, and if not altered the nature, yet lessened or increased the goodness or badness of them? And how easy is this to Him who is "about our bed, and about our path, and spieth out all our ways!" We know "the darkness is no darkness to Him, but the night shineth as the day."

6. Yea, He will bring to light, not the hidden works of darkness only, but the very thoughts and intents of the hearts. And what marvel? For He "searcheth the reins and understandeth all our thoughts." "All things are naked and open to the eyes of him with whom we have to do." "Hell and destruction are before him without a covering. How much more the hearts of the children of men!"

7. And in that day shall be discovered every inward working of every human soul; every appetite, passion, inclination, affection, with the various combinations of them, with every temper and disposition that constitute the whole complex character of each individual. So shall it be clearly and infallibly seen, who was righteous, and who was unrighteous; and in what degree every action, or person, or character was either good or evil.

8. "Then the King will say to them upon his right hand, Come, ye blessed of my Father. For I was hungry, and ye gave me meat; thirsty, and ye clothed me." In like manner, all the good they did upon earth will be recited before men and angels; whatsoever they had done, either in word or deed, in the name, or for the sake, of the Lord Jesus. All their good desires, intentions, thoughts, all their holy dispositions, will also be then remembered; and it will appear, that though they were unknown or forgotten among men, yet God noted them in His book. All their sufferings likewise for the name of Jesus, and for the testimony of a good conscience, will be displayed unto their praise from the righteous Judge, their honor before saints and angels, and the increase of that "far more exceeding and eternal weight of glory."

9. But will their evil deeds too (since, if we take in his whole life, there is not a man on earth that liveth and sinneth not), will these be remembered in that day, and mentioned in the great congregation? Many believe they will not; and ask, "Would not this imply, that their sufferings were not at an end, even when life ended?—seeing they would still have sorrow, and shame, and confusion of face to endure." They ask farther, "How can this be reconciled with God's declaration by the Prophet—'If the wicked will turn from all his sins that he hath committed, and keep all my statutes, and do that which is lawful and right; all his transgressions that he hath committed, they shall not be once mentioned unto him?' (Ezek. 18:21,22). How is it consistent with the promise that God has made to all who accept of the gospel covenant—'I will forgive their iniquities, and remember their sin no more?' (Jer. 31:34). Or, as the Apostle expresses it, 'I will be merciful

to their unrighteousness, and their sins and iniquities will I remember no more?'" (Heb. 8:12).

10. It may be answered. It is apparently and absolutely necessary, for the full display of the glory of God; for the clear and perfect manifestation of His wisdom, justice, power, and mercy, toward the heirs of salvation; that all the circumstances of their life should be placed in open view, together with all their tempers, and all the desires, thoughts, and intents of their hearts: Otherwise, how would it appear out of what a depth of sin and misery the grace of God had delivered them? And, indeed, if the whole lives of all the children of men were not manifestly discovered, the whole amazing contexture of divine providence could not be manifested; nor should we yet be able, in a thousand instances, "to justify the ways of God to man." Unless our Lord's words were fulfilled in their utmost sense, without any restriction or limitation—"There is nothing covered that shall not be revealed, or hid that shall not be known" (Matt. 10:26); abundance of God's dispensations under the sun would still appear without their reasons. And then only when God hath brought to light all the hidden things of darkness, whosoever were the actors therein, will it be seen that wise and good were all His ways; that He saw through the thick cloud, and governed all things by the wise counsel of His own will; that nothing was left to chance or the caprice of men, but God disposed all strongly and sweetly, and wrought all into one connected chain of justice, mercy, and truth.

11. And in the discovery of the divine perfections, the righteous will rejoice with joy unspeakable; far from feeling any painful sorrow or shame, for any of those past transgressions which were long since blotted out as a cloud, washed away by the blood of the Lamb. It will be abundantly sufficient for them, that all the transgressions which they had committed shall not be once mentioned unto them to their disadvantage; that their sins, and transgressions, and iniquities shall be remembered no more to their condemnation. This is the plain meaning of the promise; and this all the children of God shall find true, to their everlasting comfort.

12. After the righteous are judged, the King will turn to them upon His left hand; and they shall be judged, every man according to his works. But not only their outward works will be brought into the account, but all the evil desires, affections, tempers, which have, or have had, a place in their souls; and all the evil thoughts or designs which were ever cherished in their hearts. The joyful sentence of acquittal will then be pronounced upon those upon the right hand; the dreadful sentence of condemnation upon those on the left; both of which must remain fixed and unmovable as the throne of God.

## Circumstances That Follow the Judgment

III. 1. We may, in the third place, consider a few of the circumstances which will follow the general judgment. And the first is the execution of the sentence pronounced on the evil and on the good: "These shall go away into eternal punishment, and the righteous into life eternal." It should be observed, it is the very same word which is used, both in the former and the latter clause: It follows, that either the punishment lasts forever, or the reward too will come to an end: No, never, unless God could come to an end, or His mercy and truth could fail. "Then shall the righteous shine forth as the sun in the kingdom of their Father," "and shall drink of those rivers of pleasure which are at God's right hand forevermore." But here all description falls short: All human language fails! Only one who is caught up into the third heaven can have a just conception of it. But even such a one cannot express what he hath seen: These things it is not possible for man to utter.

The wicked, meantime, shall be turned into hell, even all the people that forget God. They will be "punished with everlasting destruction from the presence of the Lord, and from the glory of his power." They will be "cast into the lake of fire burning with brimstone," originally "prepared for the devil and his angels"; where they will gnaw their tongues for anguish and pain, they will curse God and look upward. There the dogs of hell—pride, malice, revenge, rage, horror, despair—continually devour them.

There "they have no rest, day or night, but the smoke of their torment ascendeth forever and ever!" For, "their worm dieth not, and the fire is not quenched."

2. Then the heavens will be shriveled up as a parchment scroll, and pass away with a great noise: They will "flee from the face of him that sitteth on the throne, and there will be found no place for them" (Rev. 20:11). The very manner of their passing away is disclosed to us by the Apostle Peter: "In the day of God, the heavens, being on fire, shall be dissolved" (2 Peter 3:12). The whole beautiful fabric will be overthrown by that raging element, the connexion of all its parts destroyed, and every atom torn asunder from the others. By the same, "the earth also, and the works that are therein, shall be burned up" (v. 10). The enormous works of nature, the everlasting hills, mountains that have defied the rage of time, and stood unmoved so many thousand years, will sink down in fiery ruin. How much less will the works of art, though of the most durable kind, the utmost efforts of human industry—tombs, pillars, triumphal arches, castles, pyramids—be able to withstand the flaming conqueror! All, all will die, perish, vanish away, like a dream when one awaketh!

3. It has indeed been imagined by some great and good men, that as it requires that same almighty power to annihilate things as to create; to speak into nothing or out of nothing; so no part of, no atom in, the universe, will be totally or finally destroyed. Rather, they suppose, that, as the last operation of fire, which we have yet been able to observe, is to reduce into glass what, by a smaller force, it had reduced to ashes; so, in the day God hath ordained, the whole earth, if not the material heavens also, will undergo this change, after which the fire can have no further power over them. And they believe this is intimated by that expression in the Revelation made to St. John, "Before the throne there was a sea of glass, like unto crystal" (Rev. 4:6). We cannot now either affirm or deny this; but we shall know hereafter.

4. If it be inquired by the scoffers, the minute philosophers, "How can these things be? Whence should come such an immense quantity of fire as would consume the

heavens and the whole terraqueous globe?" We would beg leave, first, to remind them, that this difficulty is not peculiar to the Christian system. The same opinion almost universally obtained among the *unbigoted* Heathens. So one of those celebrated *free-thinkers* speaks, according to the generally received sentiment (the following is Dryden's translation of this quotation from Ovid):

> Rememb'ring, in the fates, a time when fire
> Should to the battlements of heaven aspire;
> And all the blazing world above should burn,
> And all the' inferior globe to cinders turn.—Edit.

But, secondly, it is easy to answer, even from our slight and superficial acquaintance with natural things, that there are abundant magazines of fire ready prepared, and treasured up against the day of the Lord. How soon may a comet, commissioned by Him, travel down from the distant parts of the universe! And were it to fix upon the earth, in its return from the sun, when it is some thousand times hotter than a red-hot cannon-ball, who does not see what must be the immediate consequence? But, not to ascend so high as the ethereal heavens, might not the same lightnings which "give shine to the world," if commanded by the Lord of nature, give ruin and utter destruction? Or, to go no farther than the globe itself; who knows what huge reservoirs of liquid fire are from age to age contained in the bowels of the earth? Aetna, Hecla, Vesuvius, and all the other volcanoes that belch out flames and coals of fire, what are they, but so many proofs and mouths of those fiery furnaces; and at the same time so many evidences that God hath in readiness wherewith to fulfill His Word? Yea, were we to observe no more than the surface of the earth, and the things that surround us on every side, it is most certain (as a thousand experiments prove, beyond all possibility of denial) that we ourselves, our whole bodies, are full of fire, as well as every thing round about us. Is it not easy to make this ethereal fire visible even to the naked eye, and to produce thereby the very same effects on combustible matter, which are produced by culinary fire? Needs there then any more than for God to unloose that secret chain, whereby this irresistible agent is now bound down, and lies quiescent in every particle of matter? And how soon would it tear the universal frame in pieces, and involve all in one common ruin!

5. There is one circumstance more which will follow the judgment, that deserves our serious consideration: "We look," says the Apostle, "according to his promise, for new heavens and a new earth, wherein dwelleth righteousness" (2 Peter 3:13). The promise stands in the prophecy of Isaiah, "Behold, I created new heavens and a new earth: And the former shall not be remembered" (Isa. 65:17); so great shall the glory of the latter be! These St. John did behold in the visions of God. "I saw," saith he, "a new heaven and a new earth; for the first heaven and the first earth were passed away" (Rev. 21:1). And only righteousness dwelt therein. Accordingly, he adds, "And I heard a great voice from" the third "heaven, saying, Behold, the tabernacle of God is with men, and he will dwell with them, and they shall be his people; and God himself shall be with them, and be their God!" (21:3). Of necessity, therefore, they will all be happy: "God shall wipe away all tears from their eyes, and there shall be no more death, neither sorrow, nor crying; neither shall there be any more pain" (21:4). "There shall be no more curse; but they shall see his face" (22:3,4); they shall have the nearest access to, and thence the highest resemblance of, Him. This is the strongest expression in the the language of Scripture, to denote the most perfect happiness. "And his name shall be on their foreheads"; they shall be openly acknowledged as God's own property, and His glorious nature shall most visibly shine forth from them. "And there shall be no night there; and they need no candle, neither light of the sun; for the Lord God giveth them light: And they shall reign forever and ever."

IV. It remains only to apply the preceding considerations to all who are here before God. And are we not directly led so to do, by the present solemnity, which so naturally points us to that day, when the Lord will judge the world in righteousness? This, therefore, by reminding us of that more awful season, may furnish many lessons of instruction. A few of these I may be permitted just to touch on. May God write them on all our hearts!

1. And, first, how beautiful are the feet of those who are sent by the wise and gracious providence of God, to execute justice on earth, to defend the injured, and punish the wrongdoer! Are they not the ministers of God to us for good; the grand supporters of the public tranquillity; the patrons of innocence and virtue; the great security of all our temporal blessings? And does not every one of these represent, not only an earthly prince, but the Judge of the earth? Him whose "name is written upon his thigh, King of kings, and Lord of lords"? O that all these sons of the right hand of the Most High, may be holy as He is holy! wise with the wisdom that sitteth by His throne, like Him who is the eternal Wisdom of the Father! No respecters of persons, as He is none; but rendering to every man according to his works; like Him inflexibly, inexorably just, though pitiful and of tender mercy! So shall they be terrible indeed to them that do evil, as not bearing the sword in vain. So shall the laws of our land have their full use and due honor, and the throne of our King be still established in righteousness.

2. Ye truly honorable men, whom God and the King have commissioned, in a lower degree, to administer justice; may not ye be compared to those ministering spirits who will attend the Judge coming in the clouds? May you, like them, burn with love to God and man! May you love righteousness and hate iniquity! May ye all minister, in your several spheres, (such honor hath God given you also!) to them that shall be heirs of salvation, and to the glory of your great Sovereign! ornaments of your country, the protectors of a guilty land, the guardian-angels of all that are round about you!

3. You, whose office it is to execute what is given you in charge by Him before whom you stand; how nearly are you concerned to resemble those that stand before the face of the Son of Man, those servants of His that do His pleasure, and hearken to the voice of His words! Does it not highly import you, to be as uncorrupt as them? to

approve yourselves the servants of God? to do justly, and love mercy? to do to all as ye would they should do to you? So shall that great Judge, under whose eye you continually stand, say to you also, "Well done, good and faithful servants: Enter ye into the joy of your Lord!"

4. Suffer me to add a few words to all of you who are at this day present before the Lord. Should not you bear it in your minds all the day long, that a more awful day is coming? A large assembly this! But what is it to that which every eye will then behold, the general assembly of all the children of men that ever lived on the face of the whole earth? A few will stand at the judgment seat this day, to be judged touching what shall be laid to their charge; and they are now reserved in prison, perhaps in chains, till they are brought forth to be tried and sentenced. But we shall all, I that speak, and you that hear, "stand at the judgment seat of Christ." And we are now reserved on this earth, which is not our home, in this prison of flesh and blood, perhaps many of us in chains of darkness too, till we are ordered to be brought forth. Here a man is questioned concerning one or two facts, which he is supposed to have committed. There we are to give an account of all our works, from the cradle to the grave, of all our words; of all our desires and tempers, all the thoughts and intents our hearts; of all the use we have made of our various talents, whether of mind, body, or fortune, till God said, "Give an account of thy stewardship, for thou mayest be no longer steward." In this court, it is possible, some who are guilty may escape for want of evidence; but there is no want of evidence in that court. All men, with whom you had the most secret intercourse, who were privy to all your designs and actions, are ready before your face. So are all the spirits of darkness, who inspired evil designs, and assisted in the execution of them. So are all the angels of God; those eyes of the Lord, that run to and fro over all the earth, who watched over your soul, and labored for your good, so far as you would permit. So is your own conscience, a thousand witnesses in one, now no more capable of being either blinded or silenced, but constrained to know and to speak the naked

truth, touching all your thoughts, and words, and actions. And is conscience as a thousand witnesses?—yea, but God is as a thousand consciences! O, who can stand before the face of the great God, even our Savior Jesus Christ!

See! See! He cometh! He maketh the clouds His chariots! He rideth upon the wings of the wind! A devouring fire goeth before Him, and after Him a flame burneth! See! He sitteth upon His throne, clothed with light as with a garment, arrayed with majesty and honor! Behold, His eyes are as a flame of fire, His voice as the sound of many waters!

How will ye escape? Will ye call to the mountains to fall on you, the rocks to cover you? Alas, the mountains themselves, the rocks, the earth, the heavens, are just ready to flee away! Can ye prevent the sentence? Wherewith? With all the substance of thy house, with thousands of gold and silver? Blind wretch! thou camest naked from thy mother's womb, and more naked go into eternity. Hear the Lord, the Judge! "Come, ye blessed of my Father! inherit the kingdom prepared for you from the foundation of the world." Joyful sound! How widely different from that voice which echoes through the expanse of heaven, "Depart, ye cursed, into everlasting fire, prepared for the devil and his angels!" And who is he that can prevent or retard the full execution of either sentence? Vain hope! Lo, hell is moved from beneath to receive those who are ripe for destruction! And the everlasting doors lift up their heads, that the heirs of glory may come in!

5. "What manner of persons then ought we to be, in all holy conversation and godliness!" We know it cannot be long before the Lord will descend with the voice of the archangel, and the trumpet of God; when every one of us shall appear before Him, and give account of his own works. "Wherefore, beloved, seeing ye look for these things," seeing ye know He will come and will not tarry, "be diligent, that ye may be found of him in peace, without spot and blameless." Why should ye not? Why should one of you be found on the left hand, at His appearing? He willeth not that any should perish, but that all should come to repentance; by repentance, to faith in a bleeding Lord;

by faith, to spotless love, to the full image of God renewed in the heart, and producing all holiness of conversation. Can you doubt of this, when you remember, the Judge of all is likewise the Savior of all? Hath He not bought you with His own blood, that ye might not perish, but have everlasting life? O make proof of His mercy, rather than His justice; of His love rather than the thunder of His power! He is not far from every one of us; and He is now come, not to condemn, but to save the world. He standeth in the midst! Sinner, doth He not now, even now, knock at the door of thy heart? O that thou mayest know, at least in thy day, the things that belong unto thy peace! O that ye may now give yourselves to Him who gave Himself for you, in humble faith, in holy, active, patient love! So shall ye rejoice with exceeding joy in His day, when He cometh in the clouds of heaven.

**CLASSIC SERMONS Series**

Classic Sermons on the Attributes of God
Classic Sermons on the Birth of Christ
Classic Sermons on Christian Service
Classic Sermons on the Cross of Christ
Classic Sermons on Faith and Doubt
Classic Sermons on Family and Home
Classic Sermons on Heaven and Hell
Classic Sermons on Hope
Classic Sermons on the Names of God
Classic Sermons on Overcoming Fear
Classic Sermons on Prayer
Classic Sermons on Praise
Classic Sermons on the Prodigal Son
Classic Sermons on the Resurrection of Christ
Classic Sermons on the Second Coming and
   Other Prophetic Themes
Classic Sermons on the Sovereignty of God
Classic Sermons on Spiritual Warfare
Classic Sermons on Suffering
Classic Sermons on Worship